Woman and Home
Favourite Recipes

Woman and Home

Favourite Recipes

Mary Meredith

and her Cordon Bleu Cookery Team

Hamlyn

London · New York · Sydney · Toronto

All photography by Gordon le Masurier
Back jacket shows Pineapple Pudding *(see page 82)*
Front jacket shows Roast Fore Rib of Beef and
Yorkshire Puddings *(see pages 40, 41)* and Crispy
Cabbage *(see page 71)*
Page 1 shows Walnut and Chocolate Gâteau
(see page 118)
Page 2 shows Poisson Julienne *(see page 27)*

Illustrations by Shirley Tourret

Published by
The Hamlyn Publishing Group Limited
London · New York · Sydney · Toronto
Astronaut House, Feltham, Middlesex, England
© Copyright IPC Magazines Limited 1979

ISBN 0 600 39461 1

Printed and bound in Great Britain by
Morrison & Gibb Ltd, London and Edinburgh

Contents

Useful Facts and Figures 6

Introduction 8

Cook's Tips 8

Soups and Starters 12

Fish and Shellfish 26

Main Courses 40

Egg and Cheese Dishes 54

Savoury Butters, Sauces and Dressings 64

Vegetables and Salads 70

Hot and Cold Puddings 82

Party Fare 103

Cakes and Bakes 114

Index 126

Useful Facts and Figures

Notes on metrication

The exact conversion of approximately 28 grams to the ounce is not a practical figure on which to work, so we convert bearing in mind the 25 gram calibration shown on popular scales, and the quantities in which one buys food. For example, we are all so used to buying a half pound block of fat that it seemed most sensible to continue in this fashion and cut a 250-gram block in half, giving 125 grams for 4 ounces.

Ounces	Recommended conversion to nearest unit of 25
1	25
2	50
3	75
4	125
5	150
6	175
7	200
8	250
9	275
10	300
12	375
16 (1 lb)	500

Note. As a general guide, 1 kg (1000 g) equals 2.2 lb or about 2 lb 3 oz. This method of conversion gives good results in nearly all cases, although in certain pastry and cake recipes a more accurate conversion is necessary to produce a balanced recipe.

Liquid measures The millilitre has been used in this book and the following table gives a few examples.

Imperial	Recommended ml
$\frac{1}{4}$ pint	150 ml
$\frac{1}{2}$ pint	300 ml
$\frac{3}{4}$ pint	450 ml
1 pint	600 ml
1$\frac{1}{2}$ pints	900 ml
1$\frac{3}{4}$ pints	1000 ml (1 litre)

Can sizes At present, cans are marked with the exact (usually to the nearest whole number) metric equivalent of the Imperial weight of the contents, so we have followed this practice when giving can sizes.

Baking tin sizes

Inches	Centimetres
6	15
6$\frac{1}{2}$	16
7	18
7$\frac{1}{2}$	19
8	20
9	23
10	25
11	28
12	30

Oven temperatures
The table below gives recommended equivalents.

°C	°F	Gas Mark
140	275	1
150	300	2
160	325	3
180	350	4
190	375	5
200	400	6
220	425	7
230	450	8
240	475	9

Notes for American and Australian users

In America the 8-oz measuring cup is used. In Australia metric measures are now used in conjunction with the standard 250-ml measuring cup. The Imperial pint, used in Britain and Australia, is 20 fl oz, while the American pint is 16 fl oz. It is important to remember that the Australian tablespoon differs from both the British and American tablespoons; the table below gives a comparison. The British standard tablespoon, which has been used throughout this book, holds 17.7 ml, the American 14.2 ml, and the Australian 20 ml. A teaspoon holds approximately 5 ml in all three countries, this is a medical spoon which is available in some households.

British	American	Australian
1 teaspoon	1 teaspoon	1 teaspoon
1 tablespoon	1 tablespoon	1 tablespoon
2 tablespoons	3 tablespoons	2 tablespoons
$3\frac{1}{2}$ tablespoons	4 tablespoons	3 tablespoons
4 tablespoons	5 tablespoons	$3\frac{1}{2}$ tablespoons

An Imperial/American guide to solid and liquid measures

Solid measures		Liquid measures	
IMPERIAL	AMERICAN	IMPERIAL	AMERICAN
1 lb butter or margarine	2 cups	$\frac{1}{4}$ pint liquid	$\frac{2}{3}$ cup liquid
		$\frac{1}{2}$ pint	$1\frac{1}{4}$ cups
1 lb flour	4 cups	$\frac{3}{4}$ pint	2 cups
1 lb granulated or caster sugar	2 cups	1 pint	$2\frac{1}{2}$ cups
		$1\frac{1}{2}$ pints	$3\frac{3}{4}$ cups
1 lb icing sugar	3 cups	2 pints	5 cups ($2\frac{1}{2}$ pints)
8 oz rice	1 cup		

Note: When making any of the recipes in this book, only follow one set of measures as they are not interchangeable.

Introduction

Favourites – what makes our favourites? Every recipe has more than one merit. Firstly perhaps we particularly enjoy a certain dish ourselves, and secondly because our good friends, who have been to our Woman and Home Cook School, have endorsed our choice. In other words the main criterion is taste. The other merits are simple to explain and fall into one or more of the following categories – speed, economy, freezing success, good looks, interesting smell or texture, ease of forward preparation, and sometimes simply that they are a little out of the ordinary.

By adding a few of our recipes to the list of your own favourites, you can widen your repertoire of everyday dishes for family cooking and try some special occasion recipes for adventurous entertaining.

Mary Meredith

Cook's Tips

Freezing

Almost all foods can be frozen, but to make best use of freezer space we want to suggest those foods which will be particularly useful to you. With that in mind, we have marked those recipes which we would freeze ourselves. If in doubt about how one of your favourite recipes would freeze, try one helping in the freezer, thaw it next day and then make your decision.

There is a great deal of ready information about freezing, somewhat less about thawing (the golden rule is *think ahead*) but very little mention of freezer maintenance. We always stress that careful management and maintenance of a freezer is very important, to get the best results from the food and to prolong the life of this valuable piece of equipment.

There are two great allies for an annual freezer sort-out. First is a wheelbarrow, which can be wheeled into the kitchen (a pram would do as well), stacked with the freezer contents, covered with newspaper and a rug, and wheeled away into a cool place. The second is a long-handled car windscreen ice scraper, which makes short work of removing thawing ice and avoids frost-bitten hands. It is also useful to have a net bag in which to pop any mysterious packets or unlabelled packs for current use. Even labelling as carefully as time permits always results in a residue of 'lost property'.

Don't forget to clean behind the freezer when it's empty!

Filling and piping

We often use a nylon piping bag with a star or plain pipe attached, not only for decoration but for speed of method. Apart from whipped cream it is useful to pipe creamed potato, meringue and choux pastry, and to pipe cake mixtures into little paper cases.

Here is a helpful hint when filling a bag. Put the piping bag, with the pipe attached, pointing downwards into an old-fashioned round grater if you have one, or a jug, and drape the sides of the bag over the edge. Only half-fill the bag with the mixture; always leave half the bag empty so that you can give it several twists above the mixture before starting to pipe. If you use the pressure from your right hand only, pressing downwards, there will be no mixture escaping upwards. Just use your other hand to help guide the pipe. Try to avoid the temptation of gripping the bag with both hands.

Sieving and blending

For especially smooth purées of fruit, vegetables or soup we use the fine plate of a Mouli vegetable mill. The coarse plate is useful for country soups where a little texture gives the soup character.

We use our blender for all kinds of ingredients; for making breadcrumbs, chopping nuts and herbs and making soups, sauces and mayonnaise.

Remember a blender does not remove pips, such as raspberry pips, nor stringy textured fibres such as those in the coarser stems of rhubarb. These may need removing afterwards by sieving.

A bouquet garni

A bouquet garni is a very simple flavouring of fresh herbs, which we use a lot. It is generally made up of one bay leaf, a sprig of thyme and a spray of parsley, or parsley stalks tied, for easy removal, with a piece of string, which can be attached to the pan handle. I find I use bay leaves and thyme from the garden all the year round, but there are numerous bouquet garni sachets in the shops filled with blends of dried herbs. Try different kinds to get subtle variations of flavour into your cooking.

Garlic

To crush garlic take one small clove, and separate it from the root. Peel off the papery skin, then slice the clove, sprinkle it with salt and crush it to a smooth cream on a board under a broad-bladed knife. If you like the flavour and use garlic a lot, have a special little wooden board for the purpose. Otherwise, wash the board carefully, first in cold water.

Garlic is always optional, but without it the traditional flavour will be lacking in some recipes.

Mushrooms

There is no need to peel cultivated mushrooms. Simply wash them in a colander under cold water. The mushrooms keep a better shape if the stalks are not removed, but just trimmed neatly. Button mushrooms can often be used whole. Cut larger mushrooms into quarters, through cap and stalk to keep the mushroom shape.

Although mushrooms freeze well, there is really no need as they are always available at a fairly consistent price.

If there is a surplus, we chop them or put them raw through the coarse plate of the Mouli vegetable mill, then fry them in a little butter to reduce the volume. Packed into small containers and frozen they are useful for soups and sauces, or as an instant omelet filling.

Onions

Large onions are easy to peel but button onions can be really tearful and tedious. However, if you cover the onions with boiling water before peeling them it makes the job quicker.

A medium-sized knife speeds slicing and chopping. An onion can be cut up in one of two ways. Start by cutting it in half from top to root, then lay each half cut side down and slice it downwards if you want it to disappear in cooking, or horizontally if you want the pieces to remain whole.

Dicing an onion evenly is easy

if you cut it in half, top to root, lay one half flat on the board and, holding the root firmly, cut it in horizontal slices from the top within $\frac{1}{2}$ in / 1 cm of the root; do not cut through the root as it holds the onion together. Then, by cutting slices across the onion, neat dice will result. (Use the root end for stock or soup.) Dice the other onion half in the same way.

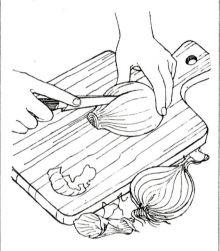

Freezing onions Peeled button onions or sliced onions are most useful in the freezer. Either should run from the container quite freely when frozen so can be kept each in a strong polythene container, clearly marked. Use from frozen.

Peeling oranges

Beautifully peeled oranges make all the difference to a fresh fruit salad. A sharp vegetable knife or a serrated knife is essential. Holding the orange firmly, slice off the top including a very little flesh, and continue cutting with a sawing action spirally round the orange, keeping your fingers below the knife as you work. It is

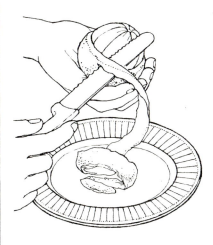

best to hold the orange over the bowl to catch any drips. By cutting through the membranes all the white pith is removed together with the outside orange peel.

For fruit salad, free each segment of flesh in turn by cutting each side of it, against the dividing membrane. For caramelled oranges the peeled oranges are usually sliced across.

Skinning tomatoes and peaches

It does not take long to skin tomatoes and is well worth while, unless they are going to be sieved.

Put the tomatoes into a bowl, pour boiling water over them and count up to 10 or 12, then lift them out of the bowl into cold water, when the skins should slip off easily after being pierced with a knife.

Peaches are also easy to peel in this way. We prefer to halve them first, as once peeled they are so slippery that it is difficult to get a grip. To halve a peach (or apricot), cut round the fruit to the stone, cutting down the

natural line, then grip it between cupped hands and twist gently to loosen the stone.

Preparing nuts
Blanching almonds This is done to remove the tough brown skins. Pour boiling water over the almonds, leave for a few minutes then drain them and slip them out of their skins. Dry them carefully. They are now ready to halve, chop, shred or grind.

To brown almonds Spread the halved, chopped or shredded almonds in the grill pan and toast them under a moderate heat for a few seconds, shaking them all the time. Alternatively, roast them in the oven at *Gas Mark 4 or 350 degrees F or 180 degrees C* for about 10 minutes.

(We prefer to brown them under the grill where it is easy to keep an eye on them as they burn very easily).

Skinning hazelnuts Toast the hazelnuts lightly under the grill or in the oven, as described for almonds. To remove the skins, rub them in a tea towel.

Peeling chestnuts There are two ways to peel chestnuts but either way start by making a deep slash in the side of each nut.

One method is to put them into a pan, bring them to the boil and simmer them for a few minutes. Take them off the heat, and when they are cool enough to handle both the outer and inner skins should peel off easily. The second method is to put them into a hot oven, *Gas Mark 7 or 425 degrees F or 220 degrees C*, for about 8 minutes. The skins will curl back and when cool enough to handle should come off quite easily.

Soups and Starters

There is no problem in choosing a first course. For instance try one of our quick but unusual hot soups – there is one to partner almost any main course and one for all seasons. With a hot starter really hot plates, soup cups or pots with lids help, especially when entertaining as it always takes guests a few minutes to gather round the table.

Fruit and vegetable starters are easy. A pâté or mousse can be prepared in advance. If you choose a cold main course you can precede it by one of our easy hot starters. Devilled mushrooms are the undisputed 'hot' favourite with readers who come to our Cook School.

Potato Soup

For 5 or 6 people
1 lb / 500 g potatoes
1 medium-sized onion
1 oz / 25 g margarine
Salt and freshly ground black
* pepper*
1 pint / 600 ml milk
1 pint / 600 ml water
1 small bay leaf
1 level teaspoon arrowroot
4 tablespoons top of the milk or
* single cream*

Peel the potatoes and the onion and slice them finely. Melt the margarine in a large pan, add the vegetables and cook them slowly, turning occasionally, for about 5 minutes. Be careful not to let them brown. Add salt and pepper, the milk, water and bay leaf. Bring the soup to the boil, cover the pan and simmer it for about 20 minutes, until the vegetables are tender, then take out the bay leaf. Sieve through the fine grid of a Mouli vegetable mill or use an electric blender. Return the soup to the rinsed-out pan. Blend the arrowroot with the top of the milk or cream and stir it into the soup; continue stirring over a gentle heat until it comes to the boil. Re-season carefully.

Variation
You can serve this soup with grated cheese or add any of the following:

Watercress Chop a washed bunch of watercress and stir into the soup just before serving.

Mushrooms Sieve or finely chop 2 oz / 50 g of washed mushrooms, add them to the soup and cook for 2 minutes.

Shrimps　　Add 2 oz/50 g of shrimps or 1 (2-oz/50-g) carton of potted shrimps to the soup just before serving.

Parsley, chervil or chives Add chopped parsley, chervil or chives to lightly flavour the soup.

Bacon Crisply fry 3 rashers of bacon, crumble them and sprinkle them over the soup.

Speedy Potato Soup Use a small packet of instant potato.

Country Carrot Soup

For 6 people
1½ lb/750 g peeled carrots,
　weighed before peeling
1 large potato, peeled
1 onion, skinned
2 oz/50 g butter
2 pints/1.15 litres light-coloured
　stock or vegetable stock
1 small bay leaf
Salt and pepper
½ pint/300 ml milk

Chop the vegetables roughly. Melt the butter in a large pan, add the vegetables and stir them over a gentle heat until the butter is absorbed. Add the stock, bay leaf, salt and pepper, bring the soup to the boil and simmer it until the vegetables are absolutely tender. Take out the bay leaf.

Sieve or use an electric blender to blend the soup, return it to the rinsed-out pan with the milk, reheat and add more salt and pepper if required.

Brussels Sprout Soup

For 8 people
1 lb/500 g Brussels sprouts
1 medium-sized potato
2 pints/1.15 litres stock (can be
　made from a stock cube)
Salt and freshly ground black
　pepper
A little grated nutmeg
A little single cream to serve
　(optional)

Cut the sprouts in half after removing any discoloured outside leaves. Peel and dice the potato. Put the sprouts and potato into a large pan with the stock, bring to the boil and simmer for about 25 minutes, until the vegetables are tender.

Allow to cool slightly, then sieve or use an electric blender and blend until it is smooth; do this in 2 or 3 batches depending on the size of the blender goblet. Alternatively, the soup may be put through a Mouli vegetable mill or a sieve. Season to taste with salt, pepper and nutmeg. Return the soup to a rinsed-out pan and reheat.

A spoonful of cream, added to each soup bowl after serving and swirled around gives a pretty effect.

Sweetcorn Soup

For 4 or 5 people

1 (12-oz/350-g) can sweetcorn
2 medium-sized potatoes
1 onion
1½ pints/900 ml stock (can be made
 from a stock cube)
A bouquet garni
½ pint/300 ml milk
Salt and pepper will only be
 required if the stock is unseasoned

Put the sweetcorn into a saucepan. Peel the potatoes and onion and cut them up roughly. Add to the sweetcorn, then pour over the stock. Add the bouquet garni, simmer the soup for about 30 minutes until the vegetables are absolutely tender. Take out the bouquet garni and then either put the soup through a vegetable mill, sieve it, or put it in the electric blender for a few seconds. Return the soup to a rinsed-out saucepan and reheat. Stir the milk lightly into the soup. Season if necessary.

Cream of Spinach Soup

For 5 or 6 people

1 oz/25 g butter
1 oz/25 g plain flour
1 pint/600 ml chicken stock
¾ pint/450 ml milk
1 (11-oz/350-g) packet frozen,
 chopped spinach
Salt and pepper

Melt the butter, remove it from the heat and stir in the flour. Add the stock and milk and stir over a gentle heat until the mixture is smooth. Bring to the boil, stirring all the time. Add the spinach, thawed or straight from the freezer, and cook gently until the soup is hot again. Season with salt and pepper.
Note: 1 lb/500 g of fresh washed spinach can be used. Cook it in the stock. Sieve or blend the soup.

Variation

Lettuce Soup Use the outside leaves of lettuce instead of fresh spinach.

Spring Onion Soup

For 6 people

2 bunches spring onions
12 oz/375 g potatoes
1 oz/25 g butter
1 pint/600 ml chicken stock (can be
 made from a stock cube)
½ pint/300 ml milk
4 tablespoons single cream
Salt and freshly ground pepper

Prepare the spring onions; keep aside the green part of two of them and chop the rest roughly. Peel and chop the potatoes and put them into a fairly large pan with the onions and butter. Cook the vegetables over a moderate heat for a few minutes. Stir in the stock and simmer the soup for about 20 minutes until the vegetables are absolutely tender. Sieve or use an electric blender to blend the soup. Put the soup back into the rinsed-out pan. Add the milk, bring it slowly to the boil, season carefully, stir in the cream and pour into hot bowls. Sprinkle each helping with the reserved green part of 2 spring onions, snipped.

Variation

Celery Soup Use 8 oz/250 g chopped celery instead of spring onions.

Curried Parsnip Soup

For 8 people
*1 large parsnip (about
    1 lb/500 g)*
1 medium-sized onion
1 clove of garlic
2 oz/50 g butter
2 level tablespoons flour
1 level teaspoon curry powder
*2 pints/1.15 litres stock (can be
    made from a stock cube)*
*Salt and freshly ground black
    pepper*
4 tablespoons single cream

Peel and slice the parsnip. Peel and chop the onion, crush the garlic. Melt the butter in a large pan, add the parsnip, onion and garlic and cook them gently together for about 10 minutes. Stir in the flour, curry powder and stock, and stir over a gentle heat until the soup comes to the boil; simmer it for about half an hour until the vegetables are tender.

Use an electric blender to blend the soup in batches or put it through a sieve or a Mouli vegetable mill. Return the soup to the rinsed-out pan, season carefully with salt if necessary and freshly ground black pepper. Add the cream and reheat to serve.

Tomato and Pumpkin Soup

For 12 people
*1 lb/500 g peeled and seeded
    pumpkin*
2 oz/50 g margarine
12 oz/375 g potatoes
1 (14-oz/396-g) can tomatoes
*2 pints/1.15 litres stock (can be
    made from a stock cube)*
*Salt and freshly ground black
    pepper*
2 tablespoons single cream
A little chopped parsley

Cut the pumpkin into a small dice. Melt the margarine in a large pan, add the pumpkin and cook over a gentle heat for about 5 minutes. Meanwhile, peel and slice the potatoes. Add them to the pan and cook for a further few minutes. Add the tomatoes, the stock and salt and pepper. Bring to the boil, cover and simmer very gently for one hour. Allow to cool slightly before blending it in several batches or put it through a Mouli vegetable mill or sieve. Return the soup to the rinsed-out pan, stir in the cream, re-season if necessary and bring back to the boil. Sprinkle each helping with a little chopped parsley before serving.
Note: Swede may be used instead of the pumpkin.

Quick Asparagus Soup

For 4 or 5 people
1 (12-oz/350-g) can asparagus
spears
¾ pint/450 ml milk
¼ pint/150 ml chicken stock (can be
made from a stock cube)
Salt and pepper

Open the can of asparagus, cut off just the tips and keep them for the garnish. Chop the rest roughly and put them into a blender goblet with the milk, stock, salt and pepper. Blend until smooth. Heat and add the asparagus tips just before serving. *Note:* This soup can be served chilled.

Artichoke Soup

For 6 people
1 lb/500 g Jerusalem artichokes
1 potato, peeled and sliced
1 pint/600 ml water
¼ pint/300 ml milk
Salt and freshly ground black
pepper
A little single cream

Peel the artichokes and put them and the sliced potato straight into the water in a fairly large pan. Bring to the boil and simmer for about 20 minutes until both vegetables are quite soft. Skim the surface of the pan if necessary, then use an electric blender to blend the vegetables until they are quite smooth or put them through a Mouli vegetable mill or sieve. Add the milk and season well with salt and freshly ground pepper. Bring back to the boil, then stir a little cream into each helping when serving. Serve with Melba toast (see page 22).

Ten-Minute Soup

For 6 people
1 lb/500 g mixed prepared
vegetables; these can be a
selection of potato, carrot, onion,
celery, cabbage, swede and
parsnip
A chicken stock cube
1½ pints/900 ml hot water
Salt and pepper
1 level tablespoon chopped parsley

Cut the vegetables into chunks and place in a blender goblet with enough of the hot water and blend until smooth. Put the blended vegetables into a fairly large pan with the rest of the water and the stock cube and bring them to the boil. Stir and simmer for 10 minutes. Season the soup with salt and pepper and sprinkle the surface of each helping with chopped parsley just before serving. *Note:* If you have no blender, chop the vegetables, cook the soup as described then put it through a Mouli vegetable mill, or sieve it.

Brown Bean Soup

Makes a substantial main-course soup.

For 5 to 6 people
8 oz/250 g brown borlotti beans
2 onions
3 tablespoons dripping or oil
1 clove of garlic
2 level tablespoons flour
2 level tablespoons tomato purée
3 pints/1.75 litres good jellied
  brown stock or 3 pints/1.75 litres
  water and stock cubes
A bouquet garni
Salt and freshly ground black
  pepper

Cover the beans with cold water and leave to soak overnight. Peel and chop the onions, melt the dripping or oil in a large pan, and soften the onions in it.

Crush the garlic and add it with the flour and tomato purée to the pan. Stir well until thoroughly mixed.

Drain the beans, and add with the stock or water and bouquet garni to the pan. Bring to the boil, skim the surface, cover the pan and simmer gently for 2 to 2½ hours, until the beans are absolutely tender. Do not add salt to the water until the beans are completely cooked, or the skins will toughen.

Remove the bouquet garni and season to taste with plenty of salt and freshly ground black pepper. Serve with a good slice of wholemeal bread.

Scotch Broth

For 6 or 8 people
3 large carrots, scraped
1 small white turnip, peeled
1 medium-sized leek, slit and
  washed
8 oz/250 g scrag end or a breast of
  lamb or flank of beef
2 oz/50 g pearl barley
3½ pints/2 litres water
Salt and pepper
A little chopped parsley

Dice two of the carrots and the turnip finely, place the third carrot in cold water. Cut the leek into ½-inch/1-cm lengths.

Put the meat into a pan and add the diced vegetables, leek, pearl barley and water. Bring the broth to the boil, skim the surface, add salt and pepper. Adjust the heat so that the broth simmers steadily, cover and cook for 2½ hours so that the bones flavour the broth. Grate the remaining carrot, add this to the broth and simmer for a further 10 to 15 minutes. Re-season and add a little more water if the broth is too thick. Take out the bones and sprinkle the surface of the broth with chopped parsley.

Rillette of Pork

This is one of the first courses readers liked on our cooks' tour of Normandy and Brittany. The hotel we stayed at has won many awards for its particular recipe, and we can all enjoy it, perhaps for a special tea by the fire. Rillette is like potted pork and is eaten with toast; no butter is needed as it is so rich. It keeps well in the refrigerator and freezes well too, so it is a good idea to make this fairly large quantity.

For 8 people
2 lb / 1 kg belly of pork
Salt and freshly ground black
pepper
1 clove of garlic
A bouquet garni

Cut the rind and bones from the pork with a sharp knife. Cut the meat into small strips, put them into an earthenware casserole and season with salt and pepper. Crush the garlic. Stir it into ¼ pint/150 ml of water, then pour this round the pork. Add the bouquet garni and cover the dish with a lid. Cook the pork very gently in a slow oven, at *Gas Mark 1 or 275 degrees F or 140 degrees C*, for 4 hours.

Drain the meat in a sieve over a large bowl, remove the bouquet garni. Shred the drained meat with two forks or mince it coarsely; it should be fairly soft and easy to do. Put the meat into pots, re-seasoning it carefully if necessary, then cover it with the melted fat which has drained from the meat. Leave to set, then store, covered with a lid, in the refrigerator.

Take the rillette out of the refrigerator about 2 hours before using so that it has time to soften to a spreading texture.

Liver Sausage and Cream Cheese Pâté

For 4 to 5 people
4 oz / 125 g liver sausage
4 oz / 125 g cream cheese
1 oz / 25 g butter, softened
A good pinch of curry powder
1 teaspoon Worcester sauce
1 tablespoon sherry
1 tablespoon double cream or
evaporated milk
Thin toast and butter to serve with
the pâté

Remove the skin from the liver sausage, then put it into a basin with the cheese and butter and beat them together until they are thoroughly mixed. Stir in the curry powder, Worcester sauce, sherry and cream or evaporated milk. Pack the pâté into small dishes and mark the surface of each with the blade end of a palette knife. Serve with thin toast and butter.
Note: The pâté will keep for several days in the refrigerator. If you decide to keep it in this way, melt a little butter and run it over the surface to prevent the pâté from drying.

Long Leeks (see page 24)

Globe Artichokes

These are really the bud of a very large thistle and have a hairy 'choke' inside which should not be eaten, though the base below it is the most delicious part of the artichoke.

Choose even-sized, fresh green artichokes which are not too large and allow one for each person. Wash them well in several changes of cold water and cut off the stalks found at the base.

Have ready a large pan of slightly salted boiling water, put in the artichokes, points facing downwards, and boil without a lid. The boiling time has to be judged according to their size and maturity; the smaller, young artichokes will cook in about 20 minutes but larger ones could take anything up to 45 minutes. The artichokes are ready when a leaf will pluck out easily.

Serving
Drain the artichokes well on absorbent kitchen paper, arrange them across the centre of a hot dish and serve plenty of melted butter separately. Give each person a deep soup plate for his artichoke – this provides a well for the melted butter and a ledge for the discarded leaves.

Eating
Pour melted butter over each artichoke when it is on the soup plate. If you like you can tilt the plate up and rest it on a knife or fork so that the butter runs to one side. Pull off each leaf and dip the base into the butter before eating just the fleshy base. You will gradually approach the thistly centre; using a small knife and fork cut out and discard this, and eat only the best part, the heart, which is underneath.

Sweetcorn

Choose heads of corn which are well filled to the tips but not too mature; the kernels should be firm but not hard. Remove the outside green sheath leaves and the silk which clings round the cob.

Put the prepared cobs in a pan of unsalted boiling water and boil them rapidly for about 20 minutes; a roasting tin with a lid could be used for this. Add 2 teaspoons of salt for the last two minutes of cooking time. Put large knobs of butter, salt and pepper into individual serving dishes and warm them.

Take out the cobs and drain on absorbent kitchen paper, and serve in the warmed dishes.

Serving
Remember to have paper napkins and finger-bowls ready. Special little sweetcorn skewers which pierce into each end of the cob or alternatively cocktail sticks can be used. Small sweet-sized paper cases can be put on the ends of the cobs to protect your fingers from the melted butter.

Eating
Run the butter over the sweetcorn, pick it up by the skewers and just gnaw!

Marinated Mushrooms (see page 25)

Avocado Vinaigrette

For 4 people
2 ripe avocados
4 lettuce leaves
¼ pint/150 ml French dressing
  (see page 67)

Just before serving, cut each avocado in half round the stone with a stainless steel or silver knife. Twist the fruit gently between the palms of your hands to separate the two halves. Take out the stone. Balance the avocado halves on lettuce leaves in small dishes and fill the centres with the French dressing.

Creamy Avocado Starter

For 6 people
2 small ripe avocados
1 (10-oz/298-g) can consommé
  soup
1 tablespoon lemon juice
1 (5-oz/142-ml) carton natural
  yoghurt
Salt and freshly ground black
  pepper
A little lemon rind, grated
Crisp biscuits or Melba toast
  (see right)

Carefully remove the outer skin, which should peel easily from a ripe avocado. Chop the flesh roughly and put it into the blender goblet with the consommé, lemon juice, yoghurt and salt and pepper. Blend until smooth. Adjust the seasoning if necessary, then divide the mixture between small pots. Allow to chill in the refrigerator for a few hours until lightly set. Sprinkle a little lemon rind over each pot and serve with crisp biscuits or Melba toast.

Melba Toast

For 6 people
6 slices of medium-sliced bread

Toast the bread on both sides. Cut off all the crusts, then slit down between the toasted sides with a sharp knife. Return the toasts to the grill, untoasted sides up, and toast until brown and curly.
  Store in an airtight container.

Peppermint Grapefruit

Halve 3 grapefruit and, using a sharp knife, loosen the sections, cutting each side of each dividing membrane. Crumble a soft white peppermint fondant over each grapefruit and if you have it put a sprig of mint in the centre, or you could use a small rose geranium leaf.
Note: If you have serrated-tipped grapefruit spoons there is really no need to prepare the sections of grapefruit.

Grilled Grapefruit

Run 1 teaspoon of sweet sherry or cherry brandy over each prepared grapefruit half. Cover the surface of the grapefruit with demerara sugar and put the halves under a fairly hot grill to brown the surface lightly and melt the sugar.

Curry Baked Eggs

For 6 people
1 sharp-flavoured dessert apple
2 oz/50 g butter
1½ level teaspoons curry powder
6 eggs
3 tablespoons single cream
Freshly ground black pepper
6 small individual ovenproof
  dishes

Peel and slice the apple and lay 2 fairly thin slices in the base of each dish. Dot each with a knob of butter then sprinkle ¼ level teaspoon of curry powder over each one. Bake in a fairly hot oven, *Gas Mark 6 or 400 degrees F or 200 degrees C*, for 10 to 15 minutes, until the apple is just tender. Break an egg into each dish, run 2 teaspoons of cream on top of each egg and sprinkle with freshly ground black pepper. Return to the oven for 7 to 10 minutes until the eggs are just set.

Tomato and Fennel Salad

(Illustrated on page 29)

Excellent served with cheese straws.

For 6 people
8 oz/250 g tomatoes
2 medium-sized fennel roots
3 tablespoons oil
1 tablespoon wine vinegar
Salt and freshly ground black
  pepper
A pinch of caster sugar
A pinch of dry mustard

Cut each tomato into 4, or 8 segments if they are large ones. Wash the fennel, cut across the root into fairly fine rings and mix it with the tomatoes. Put the oil, vinegar, salt, freshly ground black pepper, sugar and mustard into a bowl and whisk them well together; pour the dressing over the tomatoes and fennel.

The feathery top of the fennel root can be used to garnish the salad, or a few fennel seeds can be scattered over the top.

Long Leeks

(Illustrated on page 19)

The leeks are blanched and coated with a vinaigrette dressing.

For 4 people
5 medium-sized leeks
3 tablespoons oil
1 tablespoon lemon juice
Salt and freshly ground black
  pepper
A pinch of dry mustard
A pinch of caster sugar
1 tablespoon chopped parsley
Melba toast (see page 22)

Wash the leeks very well and cut off the roots. Trim the green tops but leave as much as possible. Blanch by plunging them into a large pan of boiling salted water and, when the water has returned to the boil, allow them to boil for 5 minutes. Drain and rinse under a cold tap, then drain again and slit each leek carefully in half lengthwise. Arrange on the serving dish.

Next make the dressing. Put the oil, lemon juice, salt and freshly ground black pepper, with the mustard and the sugar, into a small screw-topped jar. Shake the ingredients together until they are thoroughly mixed, then pour the dressing over the leeks and sprinkle with chopped parsley. Serve with Melba toast.

Devilled Mushrooms en Cocotte

For 4 people
1 oz/25 g butter
8 oz/250 g button mushrooms
¼ pint/125 ml soured cream
1 tablespoon tomato ketchup
1 teaspoon Worcester sauce
½ level teaspoon dry mustard
Salt and pepper
4 individual ovenproof ramekin
  dishes

Melt the butter in a small frying pan. Cut the mushrooms into quarters, and fry briskly in the butter. Divide the mushrooms between the dishes, and mix all the other ingredients together. Spoon the sauce over the mushrooms, and bake in a fairly hot oven, *Gas Mark 6 or 400 degrees F or 200 degrees C*, for about 10 minutes.

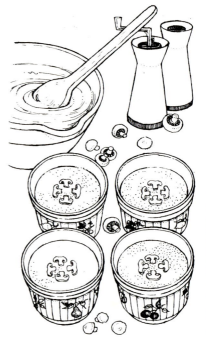

Marinated Mushrooms

(Illustrated on page 20)

For 6 people
1 lb | 500 g button mushrooms
1 tablespoon lemon juice
1 small onion or shallot
4 tablespoons wine vinegar
1 bay leaf
4 tablespoons cooking oil
1 tablespoon tomato ketchup
A good pinch of mixed herbs
Salt and freshly ground black pepper

Wash the mushrooms (there is no need to peel them), put them in a large pan with the lemon juice and cover with water. Bring to the boil and simmer for 2 to 3 minutes, then drain and allow to cool.

Chop the onion finely and put it into a small pan with the vinegar and bay leaf. Bring to the boil and simmer gently for 5 minutes. Remove from the heat and add the oil, tomato ketchup, herbs and plenty of salt and freshly ground black pepper. Mix well and pour the dressing over the mushrooms; leave them in the refrigerator to chill for several hours before serving, perhaps with fingers of bread and butter.

Asparagus Mousse

For 6 people
A few drops of cooking oil
A straight-sided 1¼-pint | 750-ml dish
½ oz | 15 g gelatine
¼ pint | 150 ml chicken stock (can be made from a stock cube)
1 (10-oz | 283-g) can cut asparagus spears
¼ pint | 150 ml plus 4 level tablespoons mayonnaise
Salt and freshly ground black pepper if needed
1 egg white

Rub a few drops of cooking oil round the inside of the dish; this will help the mousse to turn out easily.

Put the gelatine into a pan with the chicken stock and stir it over a gentle heat until the gelatine has melted; then leave it on one side to cool.

Open the can of asparagus and reserve 5 neat pieces for the top. Chop remainder. When the gelatine mixture is almost cold stir it into the mayonnaise and add the asparagus. Season with salt and freshly ground black pepper. Whisk the egg white stiffly then fold it very lightly into the mixture, turn it into the oiled dish and leave to set.

Turn the mousse on to a dish and decorate the top with the reserved asparagus spears. Serve with plain water biscuits or brown bread and butter.

Fish and Shellfish

The speed with which fish cooks is one of its greatest assets; in fact, the greatest of care has to be taken not to overcook it.

The variety of flavour, texture and colour which perfectly cooked fish can give to the menu makes it well worth a shopping search. Fish also freezes well and packs economically into a freezer, ready to make a speedy meal from frozen. When freezing fresh fish a worthwhile tip is to separate each fish or fillet carefully with freezer film so that it can be taken out separately and will thaw quickly.

The simple methods of cooking fish are often the best. In this connection, have a look through our selection of sauces and savoury butters. For example, try baked lemon cod with buttered egg sauce, or grilled sprats with mustard butter.

Cod au Gratin

For 4 people
4 frozen cod steaks
¾ pint/450 ml milk
1½ oz/40 g margarine
1½ oz/40 g plain flour
Salt and pepper
6 oz/175 g cheese, grated

Put the cod, which can be still frozen, into an ovenproof dish. Put the milk, margarine and flour into a saucepan and stir the sauce over a gentle heat until it is smooth. Increase the heat and continue to stir until the sauce thickens, then boil it for a minute or two. Season with salt and pepper and beat in three-quarters of the cheese. Coat the fish with the sauce and sprinkle the rest of the grated cheese on top.

Bake the fish in a moderate oven, *Gas Mark 4 or 350 degrees F or 180 degrees C*, for about 30 minutes or a little longer; the time will depend upon whether the fish is frozen when you start cooking. Serve with frozen peas or petits pois, cooked as directed on the packet.

Poisson Julienne

(Illustrated on page 2)

For 4 to 6 people

FOR THE PASTRY CRESCENTS

*1 (7½-oz/200-g) packet frozen
  puff pastry, thawed
A 2-inch/5-cm round fluted cutter
1 egg, beaten*

FOR THE SAUCE

*1 medium-sized onion
1 oz/25 g butter
1 lb/500 g carrots
1 wine glass white wine
1 level teaspoon plain flour
¾ pint/450 ml chicken stock
1 bay leaf
1 sprig of thyme
Salt and freshly ground black
  pepper*

FOR THE FISH

*2¼ lb/1.25 kg huss or rock salmon
2 oz/50 g plain flour seasoned with
  salt and pepper
2 tablespoons oil
1 oz/25 g butter
Chopped parsley*

Roll out pastry on a floured board to about ¼ inch/5 mm thick. Use the cutter to stamp out crescents of pastry. Re-roll the scraps and use to make more crescents.

Place them on a baking tray and brush the tops with beaten egg to glaze. Bake them in a hot oven at *Gas Mark 7 or 425 degrees F or 220 degrees C*, for 10 minutes until puffed and golden brown.

This amount of pastry makes about 32 crescents. They store well in an airtight tin; reheat before serving.

To make the sauce Peel and finely chop the onion. Melt the butter in a large frying pan and cook the onion over a low heat

for a few minutes. Peel the carrots and shred them coarsely. Add to the frying pan with the wine and cook for a few minutes to evaporate the liquid and concentrate the flavour.

Sprinkle in the flour, add the stock, bay leaf and thyme. Bring to the boil, add salt and pepper and simmer over a low heat for about 10 minutes.

To finish the dish Cut the bones from the fish. Cut the fish into 2-inch/5-cm pieces and toss in the seasoned flour, a few pieces at a time.

Melt the butter with the oil in another frying pan and cook the fish a few pieces at a time, turning them in the fat until they are golden brown. Transfer the fish to the sauce and ensure that the mixture is thoroughly heated through. Turn on to a warmed serving dish, sprinkle with parsley and garnish with pastry crescents.

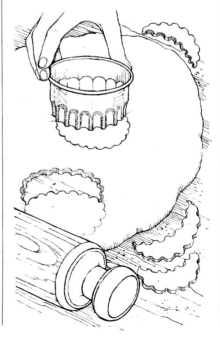

Piquant Grilled Plaice

For 2 people
1 medium-sized plaice, filleted and
with the black skin removed
2 tomatoes, halved
1 oz/25 g butter, melted
Salt and pepper
About 1 tablespoon mayonnaise

Brush both sides of the fish and the cut tomatoes with melted butter and sprinkle lightly with salt and pepper. Grease the bars of the grill pan grid and lay the fish on it, skinned side uppermost, with the tomato halves beside them. Cook under a moderate heat for 2 to 3 minutes then turn the fillets with a fish slice. Spread a little mayonnaise over each fillet and grill them for a further 2 to 3 minutes. The time required depends on the thickness of the fillets. Serve the fillets with the tomatoes and a green salad, potato crisps and wedges of lemon.

Hasty Plaice

For 4 to 5
1 (13-oz/375-g) packet frozen
plaice fillets
1 (2-oz/50-g) carton potted
shrimps
A knob of butter
½ large cucumber
Salt and pepper

Rub a flat ovenproof dish with butter then arrange the fillets of plaice on it, overlapping slightly. Put a small spoonful of potted shrimps on each one. Dot with butter. Bake the fish in a moderately hot oven, *Gas Mark 5 or 375 degrees F or 190 degrees C*, for about 10 minutes; if the fish is still frozen it may take a little longer.

Dice the cucumber, put it into a pan with enough water almost to cover it, season with salt and pepper and simmer it for 5 minutes. Drain the cucumber and arrange it at both ends of the fish.

Tomato and Fennel Salad (see page 23)
Overleaf *Tuna and Lentil Salad (see*
page 37)

28

Grilled Sprats

For 4 people
1½ to 2 lb/750 g to 1 kg sprats
Cooking oil
Fennel seed or the chopped ferny
   tops of fresh fennel, or dried dill
Salt and freshly ground black
   pepper
Brown bread and butter
1 lemon
FOR AN ACCOMPANYING
SALAD
Sliced fresh root fennel
French dressing (see page 67)

Wash the sprats, drain thoroughly in a colander and pat them dry with a piece of kitchen paper. Brush the grill pan grid with cooking oil and lay the sprats on the grid, head to tail in neat rows. Brush the fish with a little cooking oil and scatter the fennel seed over them; 1 to 2 level teaspoons should be enough for this amount of fish. Season with salt and freshly ground black pepper. The fish should be cooked at the last minute; they will have to be cooked in batches so have an oven on in which to keep the first batch hot.

When ready to cook the sprats, grill them under a hot grill for 2 to 3 minutes until they are golden brown then turn them over, brush them again with oil and the seasonings and grill for 2 to 3 minutes. Keep them hot while cooking the remaining fish in the same way.

Serve the fish very hot with freshly cut brown bread and butter and lemon wedges. Sliced root fennel tossed in French dressing makes a good accompanying salad.
Note: Whitebait can be cooked in the same way. If the bars of the grill tray are too wide to hold these tiny fish, they can be cooked in the base of the grill pan.

Crispy Bacon and Herring Roes

For 2 people
10 soft herring roes
2 rashers streaky bacon
3 oz/75 g butter
2 large slices brown bread,
   thickly cut
Salt and pepper
2 wedges of lemon

Wash and dry the soft herring roes then cut the rind off the bacon and snip the bacon into small pieces with a pair of scissors. Melt half the butter in a frying pan, then add the roes and bacon and toss over a moderate heat for a few minutes.

Meanwhile, toast the bread on both sides and spread one side with the remaining butter. When the roes and bacon are golden brown, turn them on to the buttered toasts. Sprinkle them lightly with a little salt and pepper and serve each with a wedge of lemon.
Note: You can use sliced fresh boiled cod roe in the same way.

Moules Marinières (see page 38)

33

Quick Kedgeree

For 2 or 3 people
1 small (7½-oz/212-g) packet
  quick-frozen skinless haddock
  or cod fillets or smoked haddock
¼ pint/150 ml milk
4 oz/125 g long-grain rice
2 hardboiled eggs
A little chopped parsley
1 oz/25 g butter
Salt and pepper

Put the fish into a pan with the milk and cook very slowly over a gentle heat, with the lid tightly on the pan. When the fish is tender, flake it with a fork. The remaining liquid will keep the kedgeree moist. Meanwhile put the rice into plenty of boiling water and boil it rapidly until a grain will rub away between the fingers.

Drain the rice and pour a little boiling water through it to separate the grains. Chop one of the hardboiled eggs and add it to the fish with the rice, chopped parsley and butter. Stir the kedgeree over a gentle heat until it is thoroughly hot; this will only take a very few minutes as both the fish and rice are already hot.

Season the kedgeree with salt and pepper, then garnish it with the other hardboiled egg, cut into quarters.

Smoked Haddock Pancakes

For 4 or 5 people
11 pancakes (see page 86)
1 (7-oz/200-g) packet frozen
  boil-in-the-bag buttered smoked
  haddock
Milk to make up ½ pint/300 ml
  of liquid
1 oz/25 g margarine
1 oz/25 g plain flour
Salt if necessary, pepper and a
  sprinkling of ground mace
A little melted butter

Make pancakes (see page 86), keep warm. Cook the haddock in the bag until just tender, drain off the liquid and make it up to ½ pint/300 ml with milk. Flake the fish.

Melt the margarine in a saucepan, take it off the heat and stir in the flour. Add the liquid and stir the sauce over a gentle heat until it comes to the boil, then add the flaked fish, salt and pepper and a pinch of ground mace.

Put 1 tablespoon of the mixture down the centre of each pancake. Then fold the pancake over to enclose the filling. Arrange the pancakes in an ovenproof dish and brush them with a little melted butter. Heat them thoroughly in a fairly hot oven, *Gas Mark 6 or 400 degrees F or 200 degrees C*, for about 10 minutes. The butter prevents them from drying while they heat. Serve with a green salad.

Note: The smoked haddock pancakes can be frozen. If they are reheated from completely cold or frozen they will require longer.

Smoked Haddock Lasagne

Four times this amount will fill two fairly large roasting tins and is ample when entertaining for twenty-five people.

We use the lasagne straight from the packet; it cooks well in the thin sauce, a good deal of the liquid being absorbed by the lasagne during cooking.

For 6 people
1 lb / 500 g smoked haddock fillet
1 pint / 600 ml milk
1 bay leaf
A sprig of parsley
Freshly ground black pepper
½ oz / 15 g butter
½ pint / 300 ml water
8 oz / 250 g carrots, diced
8 oz / 250 g celery, diced
2 oz / 50 g margarine
4 level tablespoons plain flour
4 oz / 125 g lasagne (this can be the green lasagne verdi)
Salt, if necessary
A fairly shallow ovenproof dish or a small roasting tin

Put the smoked haddock into the ovenproof dish and pour over the milk. Add the bay leaf and parsley and sprinkle with pepper. Cover the fish and bake it in a moderate oven, *Gas Mark 4 or 350 degrees F or 180 degrees C*, for about 20 minutes. Strain off the milk, remove any bones and the skin from the fish. Meanwhile melt the butter in a pan, add the water and the diced carrot and celery. Cover and cook until they are tender. Strain the liquid into the milk and mix the vegetables lightly into the fish.

Melt the margarine in a fairly large pan, take it off the heat and stir in the flour. Add all the liquid from the fish and vegetables and stir the sauce over a gentle heat until it is smooth, then bring it to the boil, stirring all the time. Add a little salt if necessary.

Put a layer of the fish and vegetable mixture into the oven-proof dish then add a single layer of uncooked lasagne. Moisten with the sauce then add another layer of the mixture. Add another layer of lasagne and cover with the remaining fish and vegetable mixture. Coat with the rest of the sauce. The weight of the mixture keeps the lasagne in the sauce while it cooks. Bake the lasagne in a moderately hot oven, *Gas Mark 5 or 375 degrees F or 190 degrees C*, for about 30 minutes. If you make the lasagne early in the day allow 1 hour for cooking from cold.

To freeze A most useful dish to freeze. Freeze before baking and thaw slowly overnight in the refrigerator. Cook as from cold.

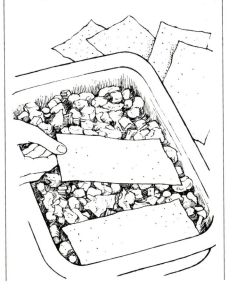

Fish Chowder

This is a thick soup; the vegetables make it enough for a main course or a substantial snack-meal.

For 8 people
1 medium-sized onion
2 sticks celery
1 oz / 25 g margarine
1 lb / 500 g potatoes
2 medium-sized carrots
1 pint / 600 ml water
1 lb / 500 g fresh haddock or cod or
  coley fillets, fresh or frozen and
  thawed
½ pint / 300 ml milk
Salt and freshly ground black
  pepper

Peel and dice the onion; wash and dice the celery. Melt the margarine in a fairly large pan, add the onion and celery and cook them very slowly for a few minutes. Peel the potatoes and carrots and dice them, then add them to the pan with the water, bring them to the boil and simmer them gently for about 10 minutes, until they are absolutely tender.

Meanwhile, skin the fish (first dipping your fingers in salt to get a firm grip) and remove any bones. Cut the fish into 1-inch / 2.5-cm cubes and add it to the vegetables. Simmer very gently for a further 8 to 10 minutes until the fish is tender. Add the milk and reheat gently. Season carefully before serving.

To freeze Freeze when cold in a polythene container; it is best thawed and reheated slowly.

Corn and Tuna Bake

For 4 people
1 (11½-oz / 326-g) can 'Mexicorn'
  (sweet corn with peppers)
1 small (7-oz / 198-g) can
  'Mexicorn' (sweet corn with
  peppers)
1 (7-oz / 198-g) can tuna fish
3 eggs
½ pint / 300 ml milk
1 tablespoon plain flour
Salt and freshly ground black
  pepper
1 oz / 25 g cornflakes
3 oz / 75 g cheese, grated
A 2-pint / 1.15-litre fluted flan dish
  10 inches / 25 cm in diameter

Mix the corn with the tuna fish then beat in the eggs, milk and flour. Season carefully with salt and freshly ground black pepper and pour the mixture into the flan dish. Mix the cornflakes and grated cheese and sprinkle them on top.

Bake in a fairly hot oven, *Gas Mark 5 or 375 degrees F or 190 degrees C,* for about 40 minutes. Serve with a coleslaw salad (see page 68).

Tuna Fish Pie

A store cupboard recipe. This dish is cooked on top of the cooker and the potato top is then warmed and browned under the grill.

For 3 people
1 oz/25 g margarine
1 oz/25 g plain flour
½ pint/300 ml milk
1 (7-oz/198-g) can tuna fish
1 (7½-oz/212-g) can button mushrooms
1 lb/500 g potatoes, cooked
Salt and freshly ground black pepper
1 oz/25 g butter, melted
A little chopped parsley
A shallow ovenproof 1¼-pint/ 750-ml dish

Melt the margarine in a pan. Take it off the heat and stir in the flour, then add all the milk and stir the sauce over a gentle heat until it thickens and comes to the boil. Open the cans and add the tuna fish and the mushrooms. Slice the potatoes. Keep the even slices for the top and put the ends into the mixture; stir this over a gentle heat until it has heated through. Season it with salt and pepper and turn it into the dish.

Lay the reserved potato slices on top, brush them very liberally with melted butter and brown them under the grill at a moderate heat. Sprinkle the top very lightly with chopped parsley.

Tuna and Lentil Salad

(Illustrated on pages 30 and 31)

This makes an excellent starter as well as an unusual salad.

For 4 people
1 (7-oz/198-g) can tuna fish
8 oz/250 g whole brown lentils
1 small onion
3 tablespoons French dressing
Salt and freshly ground black pepper

Drain the liquid from the tuna fish and flake the fish, not too finely.

Put the lentils into a large pan and cover them with cold water, then add a little salt and bring to the boil. Simmer gently for about 30 minutes until the lentils are tender, then drain them.

Peel the onion and slice it very finely into thin rings. Mix the lentils, tuna fish and onion rings together and stir in the French dressing. Season well.

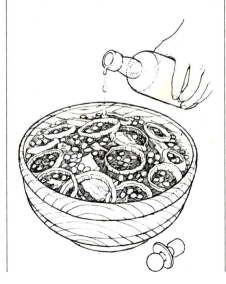

Moules Marinières

(Illustrated on page 32)

For 4 or 5 people
1 gallon/4.5 litres mussels
1 shallot
1 small onion
1 oz/25 g butter
1 clove of garlic
1 pinch of salt
4 tablespoons dry white wine
A sprig of parsley
A sprig of thyme
Chopped parsley

To clean mussels Go through the mussels carefully and discard any which are not tight shut or have cracked shells. Cover the mussels with cold water and wash them well, then pour off the water to remove some of the grit and sand. Scrape off the beard (found on the outside of the shell) with a knife. Scrape off any barnacles with a heavy, blunt kitchen knife. Wash the mussels several times more in cold water until there is no grit or sand left; they are now ready to cook.

Peel the shallot and onion and dice them finely. Melt the butter in a large pan, add the onion and shallot and cook them very gently for a few minutes. Crush the clove of garlic. Add this to the pan with the wine, parsley and thyme sprigs. Put the mussels on top, cover and cook very quickly for about 5 minutes or until all the shells are open. Using a draining spoon, lift them out of the pan on to a large dish. Take off some of the top shells, then strain the liquid over the mussels. Sprinkle with chopped parsley. If the mussels have to be kept warm for a few minutes, cover them with a cloth to help keep them moist.

To serve mussels Put the mussels for each person in a soup bowl standing on a dinner plate, which is for the empty shells. Eat with a spoon and fork, or use two joined mussel shells to grip each mussel. Use the fork for removing the mussels from the shells and the spoon (or French bread) for the juice.

Coquilles St Jacques

For 4 people
6 fresh scallops, or if these are not
*   available 1 (8-oz/250-g)*
*   packet of frozen scallops can be*
*   used*
¼ pint/150 ml fish stock or water
¼ pint/150 ml white wine
2 oz/50 g butter
1 small shallot or onion
2 oz/50 g button mushrooms
1 oz/25 g plain flour
¼ pint/150 ml milk
Salt and pepper
2 level tablespoons dry white
*   breadcrumbs*
4 deep scallop shells

The fishmonger usually cleans the scallops when he opens them; make sure the beard is trimmed away and all black parts removed.

Put the scallops into a pan with the stock or water and the wine. Simmer them very gently until they are tender; they will take about 10 minutes.

Melt the butter in another pan, chop the shallot and cook it very gently in the butter. Wipe the mushrooms (there is no need to peel cultivated ones), slice them finely and add them to the onion. Cook the mushrooms for a few seconds then take the pan off the heat and stir in the flour. Stir in the milk, then the liquid from the scallops.

Bring the sauce to the boil, stirring all the time; season it with salt and pepper. Chop the scallops, (not too finely) then add them to the sauce. Butter the shells and divide the mixture between them. Sprinkle white breadcrumbs thickly over the surface. Brown them under a moderate grill.

Crab and Cottage Cheese Flan

For 5 or 6 people
FOR THE PASTRY
6 oz/175 g plain flour
A pinch of salt
1½ oz/40 g lard
1½ oz/40 g margarine
Cold water mix
A flan tin 9 inches/23 cm in diameter, preferably with a loose base
FOR THE FILLING
¾ pint/450 ml milk
A bouquet garni
1½ oz/40 g margarine
1½ oz/40 g plain flour
2 eggs
4 oz/125 g crab meat (canned, fresh or frozen)
1 small (4-oz/125-g) carton cottage cheese
2 level teaspoons chopped chives
Salt and pepper

First make the pastry. Sift the flour and salt into a mixing bowl. Add the fats and cut them into small pieces, then rub them into the flour with the tips of your fingers. Mix with just enough cold water to make a firm dough.

Roll out the pastry on a floured board, and line the tin, trimming round the edges to neaten it. Leave the lined tin in a cool place while making the filling.

Put the milk into a pan, add the bouquet garni and bring the milk slowly to the boil to extract the flavour of the herbs. Meanwhile, melt the margarine in a fairly large pan, then take it off the heat and stir in the flour. Take out the bouquet garni and using a small whisk, whisk the hot milk on to the margarine and flour mixture. When it is smooth, stir it over a gentle heat until it comes to the boil.

Beat in the eggs, one at a time, then stir in the crab-meat, the cottage cheese, and the chopped chives with enough salt and pepper to season the mixture well. Pour this straight into the flan and put it into a moderately hot oven at *Gas Mark 6 or 400 degrees F or 200 degrees C*, for about 40 minutes.

Note: Instead of crab, you could use a small can of pink salmon, drained of the liquid.

Main Courses

Who would fault roast beef? Traditional meat-eaters will find here some of their favourite joints and main courses. Hearty poultry and mid-week recipes are at hand for reference throughout the year. I have added some unusual recipes to ring the changes and help with the housekeeping – Glazed Pork Chops, Lentil and Sausage Goulash and Drunken Bacon.

My favourite for a lazy Sunday is Devon lamb (see page 44). The gravy is made before cooking the shoulder of lamb, and the vegetables are all cooked with it. A very useful recipe for a preset oven, too.

Roast Fore Rib of Beef

(Illustrated on front jacket)

We chose roast beef for the cover of this book as it epitomises fine British food, and we selected a 5-lb/2.25-kg fore rib, enough for 8 hungry people with all the accompaniments. If there should be some left over it may be served cold with the traditional pickles.

Roasting

Put the prepared joint into a roasting tin and place in the centre of a pre-heated oven, a little higher for small joints, lower for big ones.

Ovens vary, so watch the meat carefully if you are a beginner. Take a joint out of the oven at least 15 minutes before carving, and keep it warm. This gives you time to make the gravy and it rests the meat, which will prevent shrinkage.

Pre-set oven cooking

Add 10 minutes to the calculated cooking time to allow the oven to reach the required temperature.

Gravy

Carefully spoon off all the fat leaving only the sediment remaining. Stir in 1 level tablespoon of flour for a thickened gravy and add $\frac{1}{4}$ pint/150 ml to $\frac{1}{2}$ pint/300 ml of stock, depending on the thickness of the gravy you like (gravy should not be thickened for beef or game). Season with salt and pepper.

Roast potatoes

These should be crisp and brown on the outside and light and floury in the centre.

Parboil even-sized potatoes for 5 minutes, then drain them. Meanwhile, heat 2 tablespoons of fresh dripping or white fat in a roasting tin in a fairly hot oven at *Gas Mark 5 or 6 or 375 degrees to 400 degrees F or 190 degrees C to 200 degrees C.*

While the potatoes are still hot, hold them in a tea towel and scrape the surface with a fork to make ridges, which helps them to become crisp. Put the potatoes into the hot dripping, baste and roast them for just over 1 hour, in the top of the oven. They can of course be roasted around the joint, though they may not brown quite so well, as the temperature necessary for roasting the meat is usually lower.

Yorkshire Puddings

Yorkshire Puddings are easier to serve and cook more quickly baked in a bun tin. Traditionally, however, the roast was cooked standing on a trivet in the roasting tin and the Yorkshire pudding in the tin below, catching all the sediment from the meat.

Makes 12
4 oz / 125 g plain flour
½ level teaspoon salt
1 egg
¼ pint / 150 ml milk
Scant ¼ pint / 150 ml water
A little dripping
A 12-hole bun tin

Sift the flour and salt into a bowl. Break the egg into the centre of the sifted ingredients and add the milk. Start mixing from the centre and gradually incorporate all the flour. Beat the batter well until it is smooth and shiny, then add a little water. When bubbles start to rise to the surface, stir in the remaining water.

Place specks of dripping in each bun tin and heat in the oven. Beat the batter again, then fill each tin to the top with batter. Put them into a hot oven, about *Gas Mark 7 or 425 degrees F or 220 degrees C,* for 20 to 25 minutes.
Note: If the water added is hot this cuts about 10 minutes off the total cooking time.

Mince and Onions

For 5 or 6 people
1 oz / 25 g dripping
12 oz / 375 g small onions skinned, or 2 large ones, sliced
1½ lb / 750 g raw minced beef
2 level tablespoons flour
¾ pint / 450 ml stock or water (can be made from a stock cube)
Salt and pepper

Melt the dripping, add the onions and fry them quickly until they start to colour. Add the mince and cook it quickly, breaking it up with a fork. When the mince has browned, stir in the flour and stock. Simmer for about ¾ hour. Season with salt and pepper if necessary; if using a stock cube no further seasoning will be needed.
Note: Fine or medium oatmeal can be used instead of flour. The mince can be cooked in a slow oven at *Gas Mark 2 or 300 degrees F or 150 degrees C,* for about 1 hour.

Steak and Mushroom Pie

(Illustrated on page 57)

For 6 people

1¼ lb/675 g stewing steak in one
piece

*A piece of bone marrow 2¼ inches/
6 cm long (optional)*

*8 oz/250 g button mushrooms,
rinsed*

Salt and pepper

2 level tablespoons flour

*1 (13-oz/368-g) packet frozen
puff pastry, thawed*

A little well-beaten egg

*A little boiling stock or vegetable
water*

A 2½-pint/1.4-litre pie dish

Cut the steak into 1-inch/2.5-cm
wide strips. Remove the marrow
from the bone; put a small piece
of marrow (if used) and a mushroom on one end of each strip of
steak and roll it up. Place the
empty marrow bone or a pie
funnel in the centre of the pie
dish. Mix the seasoning with
the flour, and sprinkle over the
rolls of meat. Arrange them with
the rest of the mushrooms in the
pie dish. Do not pack the dish
too tightly. Add water to come
about half way up the meat. Roll
out the pastry and cover the pie.
'Knock up' the edge of the pastry
with a round-bladed knife and
flute it.

Brush the pastry with the
beaten egg, and make a hole in
the centre over the funnel.
Decorate the top with any remaining pastry. Brush these with
egg. Bake the pie in a hot oven,
*Gas Mark 7 or 425 degrees F or 220
degrees C for 20 minutes, then reduce
the heat to Gas Mark 2 or 300*

degrees F or 150 degrees C, for a
further 1¾ hours. Cover the top
of the pie with damp greaseproof
paper if it should brown too
quickly. Just before serving the
pie, pour a little hot stock or
vegetable liquid down a funnel
in the centre of the pastry.

Note: Alternatively, 4 oz/125 g
ox kidney, with the core removed
and cut into cubes, can be rolled
in the meat with the mushrooms.

Steak and Kidney Stew

For 5 or 6 people

1½ lb/675 g chuck steak, or leg of
beef, cut in one piece

8 oz/250 g ox kidney

2 oz/50 g dripping

3 level tablespoons plain flour

*1¼ pints/750 ml stock (can be made
from a stock cube)*

*1 lb/500 g carrots, scraped and
sliced*

1 small turnip, peeled and diced

1 small parsnip, peeled and diced

2 onions, peeled and sliced

Salt and pepper, if necessary

Using a sharp knife, cut the beef
into thin slices, removing any fat
or gristle. (If you do not have a
really sharp knife ask the butcher
to slice the beef for you). Cut the
kidney in half, cut out the white
core and cut the kidney into
½-inch/1-cm cubes.

Melt the dripping in a large
pan or a frying pan and fry the
slices of meat and kidney quickly
on both sides to brown them. Stir
in the flour and stock over a
gentle heat until the mixture
comes to the boil; the gravy
should be rich brown due to the

sediment from the meat. Add the vegetables, bring to the boil and season with salt and pepper. Put it into a casserole and place it in a slow oven, about *Gas Mark 2 or 300 degrees F or 150 degrees C, for about* 1½ to 1¾ hours, or until the meat is tender.

To freeze This family stew freezes well, and is ideal for batch cooking. Freeze it in the quantities you require.

Hungarian Goulash

For 4 or 5 people
2 lb | 1 kg leg or shin beef
1 oz | 25 g plain flour
2 level tablespoons paprika
Salt and pepper
2 oz | 50 g lard or dripping
1 lb | 500 g onions
½ pint | 300 ml stock
1 (14-oz | 396-g can) tomatoes
4 tablespoons soured cream
A sprinkling of paprika

Trim and cut the meat into large cubes. Mix the flour, paprika and a good pinch of salt and pepper together and turn the meat in it to coat it evenly. Melt the fat and fry the meat quickly to brown it. Meanwhile, peel and slice the onions.

Stir the stock and any remaining seasoned flour into the browned meat. Add the sliced onion and tomatoes, with their liquid. Bring to a gentle simmer, cover and cook slowly for 2 to 2½ hours. Alternatively, cook the goulash in a covered ovenproof casserole for 2 to 2½ hours at *Gas Mark 2 or 300 degrees F or 150 degrees C.*

Spoon the soured cream over the centre of the goulash and sprinkle it lightly with paprika.

Salt Silverside of Beef

The soup, made from the vegetables and the liquid, is a bonus.

For about 8 people
4 to 5 lb | 1.75 to 2.25 kg salt silverside of beef
8 oz | 250 g carrots, scraped
8 oz | 250 g onions, peeled but left whole
1 bay leaf
10 peppercorns
½ pint | 300 ml cider
About 2 pints | 1.15 litres water or enough to cover the joint

Soak the beef in cold water overnight. Drain and put it with the vegetables into a pan which is just large enough to hold it. Add the bay leaf, peppercorns and cider. Cover the meat with water. Cook the meat in a slow oven, about *Gas Mark 3 or 325 degrees F or 160 degrees C,* for about 3 hours. Leave the joint for 1 hour to cool slightly then lift it out of the liquid. Wrap the joint in greaseproof paper, put a weight on top and leave it overnight in a cold place. Take the string off the joint before serving it.

The soup Remove the bay leaf and sieve the rest of the vegetables with the liquid or use an electric blender to blend the soup. Peeled and shredded raw tomatoes stirred into the soup at the last moment add a fresh flavour.

Family Meat Loaf

For 5 or 6 people
2 oz / 50 g white bread, without crusts
¼ pint / 150 ml milk
1 lb / 500 g raw minced beef
2 eggs, lightly beaten
1 medium-sized onion, finely diced
2 tablespoons tomato ketchup
1 teaspoon Worcester sauce
1 level teaspoon salt
Freshly ground black pepper
A 1½-pint / 900-ml loaf tin

Brush the inside of the loaf tin with a little oil or melted fat.

Crumble the bread into a mixing bowl, pour over the milk and leave for 10 minutes. Beat the minced beef into the mixture until the ingredients are evenly blended. Add the beaten eggs, finely chopped onion, tomato ketchup and Worcester sauce and stir well. Season with salt and freshly-ground black pepper.

Pack the mixture into the prepared tin and cover with a piece of greased greaseproof paper or kitchen foil. Bake the loaf just above the centre of a moderately hot oven, about *Gas Mark 6 or 400 degrees F or 200 degrees C*, for 50 minutes. If it is to be served hot, turn the loaf out immediately, otherwise leave it in the tin until it is cold. Loosen round the edges with a knife before turning it out.

To freeze Freeze whole after turning out of the tin, or in slices separated with cling film.

To thaw Thaw the whole loaf in the refrigerator overnight. Single slices will of course thaw more quickly.

Devon Lamb with Carrots and Cucumber

The gravy is made in the roasting tin before roasting the joint – no last-minute gravy making.

For 4 or 5 people
1 medium-sized leg of lamb, about 3¾ lb / 1.75 kg, or a shoulder of lamb
1 oz / 25 g dripping
4 oz / 125 g mushrooms
2 level tablespoons plain flour
½ pint / 300 ml cider
Salt and pepper
1½ lb / 675 g carrots
1 cucumber
A roasting tin with a lid or foil cover

Wipe the joint of lamb with a damp cloth. Heat the dripping in the base of the roasting tin, and brown the meat in it as evenly as possible over a fairly high heat. Take out the meat.

Wash and slice the mushrooms and fry them quickly in the roasting tin. Pour off any excess fat, leaving about 1 tablespoon in the pan.

Stir in the flour. Gradually stir in the cider and bring it to the boil. The sauce will be very thick at this stage, but will thin as the vegetables and meat cook. Sprinkle the joint with salt and pepper, and return to the roasting tin. Peel the carrots and cut them into quarters lengthways. Wipe the cucumber, divide it into three, and cut each piece into 4 lengthways. Put the vegetables around the meat and baste the meat and vegetables with the sauce; cover the tin with the lid or foil, and cook the joint in a moderate oven, *Gas Mark 4 or 350 degrees F or 180 degrees C*, for about 1 hour. Lower the heat to *Gas Mark 2 or 300 degrees F or 150 degrees C*, for a further 1 to 1½ hours. The vegetables and meat must be quite tender.

Pour the gravy from around the joint into a sauceboat. Arrange the vegetables round the meat and serve with new potatoes and green peas.

Lamb Chop Medley

For 4 people
4 lean lamb chops
8 oz / 250 g onions
12 oz / 375 g carrots
1 lb / 500 g potatoes
1 level teaspoon ground cinnamon
Salt and freshly ground black pepper
1 (15-oz / 425-g) can tomatoes

Trim any excess fat from the chops. Put the chops into a large frying pan, standing them upright on their fat edges, leaning one chop against the other for support. Fry briskly to brown the fat edges (this will make a little fat in the pan) then lay them down and fry them on both sides to brown them. Take them out of the pan.

Meanwhile, peel the onions, carrots and potatoes and slice them fairly finely. After frying the chops, put the vegetables into the pan, sprinkle them with the ground cinnamon, salt and pepper and stir them over a moderate heat for about 10 minutes. Stir in the contents of the can of tomatoes and bring the mixture to the boil. Transfer the·vegetables to an ovenproof

casserole and place the chops on top. Cover the dish with a lid or a piece of kitchen foil and cook it in a moderate oven, about *Gas Mark 4 or 350 degrees F or 180 degrees C*, for 45 minutes. Remove the lid and continue cooking for a further 30 minutes.

Breast of Lamb, Sweet and Sour

For 3 or 4 people
1 breast of lamb ; choose a thick one as it will be more meaty
FOR THE BASTE
A good pinch of salt
2 tablespoons soy sauce
2 teaspoons Worcester sauce
2 tablespoons tomato ketchup
1 level teaspoon made mustard
2 level teaspoons honey
2 tablespoons chutney

Divide the breast of lamb into strips by cutting between the bones. (The butcher will chop it for you but he might splinter the bone.)

Put the lamb into a pan, cover it with water and add a good pinch of salt. Bring it slowly to the boil and simmer for 1 minute, then pour off the water.

Mix all the ingredients for the sweet and sour baste in a roasting tin, then add the lamb and baste it thoroughly with the mixture. Cook the meat in a fairly hot oven, *Gas Mark 6 or 400 degrees F or 200 degrees C*, for 30 minutes or until the meat is crisp and golden.

Note: The ingredients for the sweet and sour baste can be very flexible; you can have fun with different flavours, or use up any little bits and pieces.

Marinated Pork Chops

For 2 people
1 orange
2 pork chops
1 level teaspoon finely grated lemon rind
1 level teaspoon finely chopped mixed fresh herbs (we used thyme and sage, but parsley could also be included)
Salt and freshly ground black pepper
A little grated nutmeg
A good pinch of paprika
A good pinch of caster sugar
Potato crisps to garnish

Cut 2 slices from the centre of the orange and reserve to put on top of the chops. Grate the rind from the remaining orange and squeeze out the juice, then mix both rind and juice with the grated lemon rind, mixed herbs, salt, pepper, nutmeg, paprika and sugar. Put the chops into the grill pan without the grid, cover them with the mixture and leave them for 30 minutes.

Cook the marinated chops under a moderate heat for about 10 minutes; turn and baste them with the marinade, cook them for a further 5 minutes, then put an orange slice on top of each. Continue grilling for a further 5 minutes – the exact times depend on the thickness of the chops, but they should be well cooked.

Serve the chops on a hot dish garnished with potato crisps and serve a green salad separately.

Glazed Pork Chops

For 2 people
2 pork chops, about 1 inch/2.5 cm thick
1 level tablespoon soft brown sugar
2 level teaspoons dry mustard
Salt and pepper
2 teaspoons lemon juice

Mix the brown sugar, dry mustard and a good pinch of salt and pepper together. Sprinkle this mixture thickly over the chops and lay them in an ovenproof dish. Sprinkle over the lemon juice.

Bake the chops in a moderately hot oven, about *Gas Mark 5 or 375 degrees F or 190 degrees C*, for 40 minutes.

Pork and Prune Casserole

(Illustrated on page 58)

For 8 people
3 lb/1.5 kg blade or shoulder of pork, boned (pie pork can be used)
1 lb/500 g button onions
4 tablespoons cooking oil
2 oz/50 g margarine
2 oz/50 g plain flour
1 pint/600 ml cider
1 pint/600 ml stock (can be made from a stock cube)
1 lb/500 g dried prunes
Salt and freshly ground black pepper
A bouquet garni
To serve with the casserole
1 green-skinned dessert apple
1 (5-fl oz/142-ml) carton soured cream
Plain boiled potatoes

Cut the meat into fairly large chunks, removing any excess fat. Blanch the onions, then remove the skins, but leave the onions whole. Melt the oil and margarine together in a large pan, add the pork and fry, a few pieces at a time, over a high heat to brown. When the meat is browned, transfer it to an ovenproof casserole.

Fry the onions for a few minutes and transfer to the casserole. Take the pan off the heat and stir in the flour. Add the cider and stock and stir the mixture over a low heat until it comes to the boil. Add the prunes, salt and pepper and the bouquet garni then pour this sauce over the meat.

Cook the casserole in a slow oven, tightly covered, at about *Gas Mark 3 or 325 degrees F or 160 degrees C*, for 2 hours. Remove the bouquet garni.

Serve the casserole with the unpeeled apple slices mixed with soured cream, and plain boiled potatoes.

Crispy Baked Pork Slices with Apples

For 6 or 7 people
2 lb / 1 kg fresh belly of pork
2 level tablespoons plain flour,
seasoned with salt and pepper
1 large egg
Browned breadcrumbs
6 or 7 small cooking apples
½ packet sage and onion stuffing
crumbs, made up as directed on
the packet

Divide the pork into thick slices by cutting between the bones. Sprinkle them lightly on both sides with seasoned flour, and coat with beaten egg and breadcrumbs.

Lay the pork on a grid (we used a small wire cooling tray) in a roasting tin. (This is important to catch the fat which comes out of the meat during the cooking; it also means the apples can be cooked beneath). Cook the pork in a fairly hot oven, about *Gas Mark 6 or 400 degrees F or 200 degrees C*, for 1 hour.

Cut the apples in half across and take out the cores with an apple corer. Place them in the roasting tin cut side facing upwards and pile the sage and onion stuffing on top of each apple half. Put the pork back on top and continue cooking them both in the oven for a further 20 minutes.

Serve the pork slices and apples on a long dish or board.

47

Red Lentils with Salt Pork

For 4 or 5 people
1 oz/25 g dripping
8 oz/250 g onions, thinly sliced
2 lb/1 kg salt belly of pork
8 oz/250 g red lentils
1 carrot, cut into quarters
1 pint/600 ml water
A bouquet garni
Pepper, and salt if required

Melt the dripping in a pan and fry the onions until they are almost tender, without browning. Add the pork to the pan and sprinkle the lentils round it; add the carrot, water and bouquet garni.

Cover and cook the pork in a slow oven, about *Gas Mark 2 or 300 degrees F or 150 degrees C*, for about 2 hours. Slice the pork before serving, remove the bouquet garni and season the lentils if necessary.

To pressure cook Use only ½ pint/300 ml of water and cook at 15 lb (high) pressure for 35 minutes.

Drunken Bacon

A cold joint for cutting at the weekend.

For 6 people
3 lb/1.5 kg collar of bacon, or a
pre-packed piece
1 onion, sliced
1 stick celery, cleaned and sliced
1 carrot, scraped and sliced
1 leek, washed and sliced
8 peppercorns
1 bay leaf
About ¼ pint/150 ml mead
FOR THE TOP
2 level tablespoons coarse mustard
1 level tablespoon cornflake crumbs

Cover the bacon in cold water and soak for 2 hours. Drain and put the bacon into a large pan. Add the onion, celery, carrot and leek to the bacon with the peppercorns and bay leaf. Just cover the bacon with cold water and bring it slowly to the boil. Skim away any scum that has gathered on the surface, cover and simmer the bacon gently for 1 hour 20 minutes. Leave it in the liquid until it is just cool enough to handle, then take it out and remove the outside skin. Press the joint into a tight-fitting dish (we used a soufflé dish). Pour over the mead, put a plate on top, then a heavy weight and leave it in the refrigerator for 2 to 3 days for the flavour to penetrate the meat. Meanwhile, the liquid and vegetables can make the base of a good soup.

Take the meat out of the dish, spread the fat with coarse mustard, then roll it in cornflake crumbs to coat.
Note: This is an ideal recipe for even a small joint. Time as for a pre-packed joint.

Lentil and Sausage Goulash

This is a complete meal in a dish.

For about 6 people
12 oz/375 g brown lentils
2 red peppers
1 clove garlic
1 tablespoon cooking oil
1 large onion, sliced
1 (14-oz/396-g) can tomatoes
Salt and pepper
1 level teaspoon paprika
*1 lb/500 g cooked sausages or
  6 frankfurter sausages*
Chopped parsley

Put the lentils in a pan with 2 pints/1.15 litres of water and boil them gently until they are tender; they will take about 45 minutes.

Cut the peppers in half, discard the seeds and slice the peppers. Crush the clove of garlic. Heat the oil in a frying pan and add the onion, peppers and garlic, cook them over a moderate heat for about 10 minutes until they are soft. Add them to the lentils with the tomatoes and their liquid. Season well with salt and pepper, and add the paprika. Stir in the sausages and heat them thoroughly in the goulash for about 15 minutes. Sprinkle the top with chopped parsley.

A lentil dish of this kind keeps hot well if it is covered. If the lentils should thicken too much, thin them slightly with a little hot stock or water.

To pressure cook Cook the lentils, without soaking them, at 15 lb (high) pressure for 10 minutes; they will then be ready to have the cooked vegetable mixture added.

If you use red lentils they will cook a little quicker.

Stuffed Liver

For 4 or 5 people
*8 to 12 oz/250 to 375 g pig's liver,
  in one piece*
Salt and pepper
1 small onion, finely diced
1 oz/25 g butter
1 level teaspoon chopped parsley
*1 level teaspoon finely grated lemon
  rind*
*1 oz/25 g freshly made white
  breadcrumbs*
2 rashers streaky bacon, thinly cut

Slice the liver horizontally, nearly all the way across. Sprinkle the inside with salt and pepper. Fry the onion lightly in the butter and mix with the chopped parsley, lemon rind and breadcrumbs. Season the stuffing with salt and pepper and pack it into the centre of the liver.

Cut the rinds off the bacon, cut the rashers in half and lay them across the top of the liver. Bake the liver in a slow oven, about *Gas Mark 3 or 325 degrees F or 160 degrees C*, for about ¾ hour. Serve with Brussels sprouts and creamed potatoes.

Kidney and Sausage Turbigo

For 3 or 4 people
8 oz / 250 g ox kidney
1 tablespoon cooking oil
4 chipolata sausages
2 medium-sized onions, skinned and sliced
4 oz / 125 g mushrooms, washed and quartered
2 oz / 50 g plain flour
¾ pint / 450 ml stock (can be made from a stock cube)
2 level teaspoons tomato purée or ketchup
1 tablespoon sherry (optional)
Salt and freshly ground black pepper
FOR THE ACCOMPANIMENT
6 oz / 175 g noodles
1 oz / 25 g butter

Cut each kidney into half, remove the central core, then cut into medium-sized cubes. Heat the oil in a large frying pan and fry the kidney gently for about 5 minutes. Take out of the pan. Twist and cut each sausage in half and fry them until they are evenly browned. Take them out of the pan and fry the onion and mushrooms for about 5 minutes, stirring occasionally. Sprinkle in the flour, then stir in the stock. Bring this to the boil then add the tomato purée or ketchup and the sherry if used. Season carefully with salt and freshly ground pepper. Return the kidneys and sausages and simmer the Turbigo very gently for 10 to 15 minutes.

The noodles
Meanwhile half fill a large pan with water and bring it to the boil. Add a level teaspoon of salt and stir in the noodles. Boil steadily for about 7 minutes, stirring occasionally until the noodles are just cooked (be careful not to overcook them). Strain the noodles in a colander. Rinse out the pan and melt the butter. Return the noodles and shake the pan over a gentle heat to coat the noodles lightly.

Turn the Turbigo into a deep dish and surround it with noodles. Serve a green salad separately.

Devilled Kidneys on Toast

For 2 people
4 lambs' kidneys
1 oz / 25 g dripping
1 small onion, finely sliced
1 level teaspoon curry powder
A squeeze of lemon juice
2 slices of toast
A little chopped parsley

Skin the kidneys, halve them and remove the central cores. Melt the dripping in a frying pan and fry the onion gently until it is tender. Add the curry powder and fry it gently for a few minutes, then add the lemon juice and the halved kidneys and cook over a gentle heat until ready. Pile the mixture on to the slices of toast and sprinkle with chopped parsley.

Pressed Ox Tongue

Partnered with a cold bacon joint, the tongue makes a good centrepiece for a cold buffet lunch.

For 8 to 10 people
1 salted ox tongue (3½ to 4 lb/
  1.5 to 1.75 kg)
2 blades mace
8 peppercorns
1 onion, cut in half
2 carrots, scraped and sliced
4 tablespoons of the liquid in which
  the tongue was cooked
A 6-inch/15-cm round tin or
  soufflé dish in which to press the
  tongue

Soak the tongue in cold water overnight then put it into a large pan with the mace, peppercorns, onion and carrots. Cover the tongue with cold water, bring it slowly to the boil and skim away any scum that has gathered on the surface. Put on the lid and simmer for 4 hours.

Take the tongue out of the liquid when it is cool enough to handle; peel off the thick outer skin and remove any small bones from the neck end. Curl the tongue into the tin or soufflé dish and add 4 tablespoons of the liquid. Cover the top with a piece of polythene or a small plate that fits exactly. Put a heavy weight on top and leave in a cool place overnight.

To turn out the tongue Dip the tin into hot water for 1 second and slip the tongue out on to a board or plate. Chill before carving across the grain in fairly thin slices. It is easiest to cut the round of tongue in half, turn it on to the cut edge and slice downwards. Serve with a cole-slaw salad.

To freeze When the tongue is peeled, line the inside of the tin with a polythene bag, press the tongue into the bag, add the liquid, close the bag and press overnight. Next day lift the tongue, still in the bag, out of the tin and put it into the freezer.

To pressure cook Cook for 15 minutes per pound (half kilo) at 15 lb (high) pressure, then peel and press as described.

Crispy Oven-Baked Chicken

For 6 people
1 oz/25 g plain flour
1 level teaspoon chopped marjoram
1 level teaspoon chopped thyme
1 level teaspoon celery salt
Freshly ground black pepper
1 large jointed chicken or 6 chicken
  joints
1 oz/25 g butter
1 tablespoon oil
¼ pint/150 ml boiling water

Mix the flour, herbs and seasoning together and sprinkle evenly over the chicken joints.

Melt the butter and heat the oil in a large pan and brown the chicken joints all over. Put the joints in a large ovenproof dish or roasting tin so that the skin side is uppermost. Sprinkle over the rest of the flour mixture, add the water and cook the chicken in a moderate oven, about *Gas Mark 4 or 350 degrees F or 180 degrees C*, for ¾ of an hour. Serve with Bean or Pasta Salad (see page 81).

Lemon Thyme Chicken

For 4 or 5 people
2 oz/50 g butter
1 chicken or 5 chicken joints
Salt and pepper
The juice and finely grated rind of
*   1 lemon*
1 large sprig of thyme
FOR THE ACCOMPANIMENT
1 lb/500 g broccoli heads
Salt and pepper
A knob of butter
1 pint/600 ml white sauce (see page
*   66)*

Melt the butter in a frying pan and fry the joints to brown them lightly. Transfer them to an ovenproof dish and sprinkle with salt, pepper and the lemon rind. Add the lemon juice to the chicken juices remaining in the frying pan and pour them all over the chicken. Add the sprig of thyme and cover the dish with a lid or a piece of kitchen foil. Cook the chicken in a moderate oven, about *Gas Mark 4 or 350 degrees F or 180 degrees C,* for about 1 hour or until the chicken is tender. Take out the sprig of thyme.

Make the white sauce.

Wash the broccoli and cook quickly in boiling salted water. When it is just tender drain it; melt the butter in the pan, and toss the broccoli gently in the melted butter with salt and pepper.

Arrange the chicken joints at one end of a serving dish and the broccoli at the other. Coat the broccoli with the sauce. Serve with new potatoes.

Note: Use frozen broccoli if fresh broccoli is not available.

Chicken Joints in Creamed Horseradish Sauce

For 4 or 5 people
1 small chicken, jointed, or 5
*   chicken joints*
2 oz/50 g margarine
1 tablespoon oil
2 oz/50 g plain flour
1 pint/600 ml chicken stock (can be
*   made from a stock cube)*
6 teaspoons creamed horseradish
*   sauce*
A little salt and pepper

Melt the margarine and heat the oil in a large frying pan. Fit in the chicken joints and fry them gently until they are golden brown; they will need about 10 minutes on each side. Take the joints out of the pan.

Stir in the flour. Add the stock and stir the sauce over a low heat until it is smooth, then bring it to the boil. Stir in the creamed horseradish sauce then season with a very little salt and pepper. Return the joints of chicken to the pan, cover with a lid or a piece of foil and simmer the joints for a further 40 minutes or until they are tender.

Serve the chicken with grilled tomatoes or runner beans or spinach.

Chicken Pot au Feu

For 6 people

1 chicken, about 4 lb / 1.75 kg
8 oz / 250 g onions, peeled and sliced
1 lb / 500 g carrots, cut into thick slices
A bouquet garni
Salt and freshly ground black pepper
1 lb / 500 g potatoes
1 lb / 500 g leeks
4 oz / 125 g mushrooms, washed
2 oz / 50 g margarine
8 oz / 250 g lean bacon rashers (we used collar bacon)
4 level tablespoons plain flour

Remove the giblets from the chicken and wash them thoroughly. Put the chicken into a very large pan with the giblets, sliced onion, carrots, bouquet garni and salt and pepper. Just cover the bird with cold water and bring it slowly to the boil then simmer gently for about 1 hour.

Meanwhile, peel and cut the potatoes into chunks, slit the leeks lengthwise, wash them well and cut them into 1-inch/2.5-cm lengths. Halve the mushrooms.

Melt the margarine then add the bacon, cut into strips, and fry it for 1 to 2 minutes. Stir in the flour than add 1 pint/600 ml of the liquid from the boiling chicken. Whisk the mixture to keep it smooth then bring it to the boil. This is now a thick sauce. Return it to the pan, add the remaining vegetables, stir well and simmer very gently for 1 hour until the vegetables and chicken are tender.

Note: This is a good way to use a boiling fowl, but allow 1 hour extra before making the sauce.

Turkey Turnover

For 6 people

1 lb / 500 g cold cooked turkey meat
8 oz / 250 g mushrooms
½ pint / 300 ml bread sauce, left over or made up as directed on a packet of bread sauce mix
Salt and pepper, if required
1 level teaspoon dried thyme
1 (13-oz / 368-g) packet frozen puff pastry, thawed
A little beaten egg for the glaze

Cut the turkey into cubes or strips. Wash and slice the mushrooms. Add the mushrooms and turkey to the bread sauce with seasoning, if necessary, and the thyme. Allow to cool if using warm bread sauce. Roll out half the puff pastry to approximately 12 inches/30 cm long by 8 inches/20 cm wide. Transfer to a baking tray, put the filling on to the pastry and spread it to within ¾ inch/1.5 cm of the edge. Roll the remaining pastry to 1 inch/2.5 cm larger all round. Brush a little water round the edges of the pastry beyond the filling, then lift the larger piece of pastry over it so that the filling is completely enclosed.

Neaten pastry edges with a sharp knife, then press the edges firmly together and knock them up with the back of the knife.

Brush the top with beaten egg then, using the back of a knife, score the top in diamonds.

Leave the turnover in a cool place for at least 10 minutes. Bake it in a hot oven, about *Gas Mark 7 or 425 degrees F or 220 degrees C,* for 20 minutes, then reduce the heat to *Gas Mark 5 or 375 degrees F or 190 degrees C,* for a further 20 to 25 minutes.

Egg and Cheese Dishes

These are the great snack ingredients but deserve much more honour. There is no one ingredient more versatile than an egg, and we hope you enjoy our main-course recipes using eggs, often combined with cheese which makes an appetising partnership.

Keeping Eggs

If bought fresh, eggs will keep well for at least 6 weeks in a cool place; turn them once a week to keep the yolks central. If you keep your eggs on a cardboard egg tray, put another tray on top and carefully turn the whole thing over each week.

Store your eggs at room temperature rather than in the refrigerator.

To get the maximum volume for baking and general cooking, it is best if the eggs are not too fresh. Egg whites will keep for 2 or 3 weeks in an airtight container in the refrigerator but yolks must always be used at once.

Note: Egg whites will whip stiffly when they are about 5 days old.

Grilled Omelet

For 4 people
8 eggs
Salt and pepper
¼ pint / 150 ml hot water
1 oz / 25 g butter
8 oz / 250 g streaky bacon, thinly cut
Chopped spring onions or chives

Break the eggs into a large basin and mix the yolks and whites lightly with a whisk or fork. Season with salt and pepper and beat in the hot water.

Melt the butter in a large omelet pan. Add the eggs and stir with a fork until the eggs begin to set. Lay the bacon on top and place under a hot grill just to cook and crisp the bacon. Scatter the top with spring onions or chives snipped with a pair of scissors.

An Omelet with a Lettuce Filling

For 1 person

A good handful of lettuce leaves washed and dried (outside leaves should be included)
½ oz/15 g butter
Salt and pepper
A pinch of caster sugar
2 eggs
An omelet pan, 6 inches/15 cm in diameter
A hot plate on which to serve the omelet

Shred the lettuce leaves roughly. Melt half the butter in a fairly large frying pan, add the lettuce and cook it over a fairly high heat, stirring all the time, for 1 to 2 minutes to reduce and cook the lettuce and evaporate the moisture. Season with salt and pepper and a pinch of caster sugar.

Meanwhile, break the eggs into a basin, add 2 half egg-shells (about 2 tablespoons) of water, add salt and pepper and beat with a fork just to break the yolks. Heat the omelet pan, add the rest of the butter and swirl it round to coat the base of the pan. Add the egg mixture and, using the fork, stir it gently, working the cooked egg from the base to the surface and letting the uncooked egg run below. While the omelet is still moist, stop stirring. Keeping it over a high heat, heap the lettuce across the centre. Flip over the side of the omelet next to the pan handle, then gripping the handle from beneath, palm upwards, tap the handle gently with your other hand to help the omelet slide towards the opposite edge

of the pan, and roll the omelet on to a hot plate.

Eat at once.

Note: The fillings for an omelet are legion. Tomato, cheese, ham, mushroom, shellfish or chopped fresh herbs can be added to the egg mixture before cooking.

Spanish Omelet

For 4 people

1 lb/500 g potatoes, peeled
1 bunch spring onions
1 small red pepper
2 tablespoons cooking oil
6 eggs
6 half egg shells of cold water
Salt and pepper
A frying pan, 8 inches/20 cm in diameter

Cut the potatoes into ½-inch/1-cm cubes. Remove the outside skins from the spring onions, and cut them across in half if they are large. Cut the red pepper in half, remove the seeds carefully and shred the pepper.

Heat the oil in a large omelet pan and fry the diced potato very slowly until it is just tender, then add the onions and pepper and fry them together until they are all tender and lightly browned.

Break the eggs into a basin, add the water, measured in a half egg shell (this is a handy measure and saves finding a spoon). Season the eggs with salt and pepper and beat them together with a fork just to break them and mix the yolks and whites lightly. Pour the eggs on to the vegetables and cook the omelet over a fairly brisk heat, stirring it to begin with, until it sets. Serve straight from the pan.

Pickled Eggs

2 pints/1.15 litres distilled white
 vinegar
2 blades of mace
12 peppercorns
4 cloves
2 small bay leaves
3 chillies, dried
18 eggs
Wide-necked jars
Porosan fruit-preserving skin
String

Put the vinegar into a pan with the mace, peppercorns, cloves, bay leaves and chillies; bring to the boil and simmer for three minutes then leave until cold.

Hardboil the eggs, then run them under cold water for 2 to 3 minutes to cool them quickly and keep the yolks a good colour. When they are cold, shell the eggs and pack them tightly into jars and cover with the cold spiced vinegar. Divide the spices evenly between the jars as they will continue to flavour the eggs. Cover the jars with Porosan skin and tie very securely under the rim of each jar with string. The covering prevents the vinegar from evaporating during storage.

The eggs will be ready to eat in 2 weeks but they will keep for 3 months or longer.

Oeufs sur le Plat (Shirred Eggs)

For 3 people
1½ oz/40 g butter
6 eggs
3 tablespoons single cream or top of
 the milk
Salt and freshly ground black pepper
Freshly cooked spring vegetables
Toast and butter to serve with the
 eggs

Divide the butter between 3 individual, shallow, ovenproof dishes or plates. Put them into a moderately hot oven, *Gas Mark 5 or 375 degrees F or 190 degrees C,* for 2 to 3 minutes to melt the butter.

Break 2 eggs into each prepared dish, spoon the single cream or top of the milk over the yolks. Sprinkle the eggs with salt and freshly ground black pepper; the whites will start to cook as soon as they touch the hot plates, so that they are certain to be set without the yolks being hardened.

Put the eggs into the oven for 3 to 4 minutes, just to set the whites; the yolks should still be creamy.

Steak and Mushroom Pie (see page 42)

Curried Egg Mousse

For 4 people
3 level teaspoons gelatine
    (this is about ½ oz/15 g)
¼ pint/150 ml chicken stock (can be
    made from a stock cube)
½ pint/300 ml mayonnaise
4 hardboiled eggs
1 level teaspoon curry paste
A few drops Worcester sauce
Salt and pepper
1 egg white
Chopped parsley
A straight-sided 1½-pint/900-ml
    soufflé dish

Sprinkle the gelatine over the stock in a small pan and leave for 1 to 2 minutes to soften. Dissolve gelatine over a very gentle heat without allowing it to boil. Cool it, and stir it into the mayonnaise. Shell 3 of the hardboiled eggs, and chop the whites. Sieve the yolks of the 3 eggs and stir them into the mayonnaise mixture with the curry paste and Worcester sauce. Season carefully. Whip the egg white stiffly and fold it lightly into the mixture, then turn the mixture into the soufflé dish.

When set, divide the surface into 5 equal sections with radiating lines of chopped parsley carefully dropped from the blade of a knife.

Shell the remaining egg and cut the white into 5 'petals'. Arrange 1 petal between the lines of parsley. Sieve the yolk and pile it in the centre. Serve with bread and butter and a green salad.

Pork and Prune Casserole (see page 46)

Cheese Soufflé

For 3 people
¾ oz/20 g margarine
¾ oz/20 g plain flour
¼ pint/150 ml milk
2 oz/50 g cheese, finely grated
Salt and a pinch of cayenne pepper
2 large eggs or 3 small ones
A straight-sided soufflé dish,
    6 inches/15 cm in diameter

Tie a double strip of greaseproof paper around the outside of the soufflé dish, to come at least 1 inch/2.5 cm above the rim. It is best not to grease the dish as the soufflé will rise better without it.

Melt the margarine in a fairly large saucepan, take it off the heat and stir in the flour, then the milk. Stir the sauce over a low heat, increasing this slightly when the sauce is smooth. Bring the sauce to the boil, and simmer for 1 minute. It is called a panada at this stage. Take it off the heat and beat in the grated cheese. Season the mixture well with salt and cayenne pepper.

Separate the egg yolks from the whites and beat the yolks into the cheese mixture. Whip the whites stiffly and fold them in. Turn the mixture into the prepared soufflé dish. Put on a baking tray and put the tray straight into a moderately hot oven *Gas Mark 5 or 375 degrees F or 190 degrees C*, for 30 to 35 minutes. The soufflé should be lightly browned on top. A hot soufflé should still be moist in the centre.

Note: Be ready to serve the soufflé immediately; this is one dish which must be eaten straight from the oven and very hot.

Piperade

This dish can be made in the pan like scrambled egg but we found it far easier to serve and more attractive when finished off by baking in the oven. That is the way Piperade is served in Riberac, a country town in the Dordogne district of France.

For 6 or 7 people double the quantities and bake the Piperade in a larger dish for 40 minutes at the temperature given.

For 3 people
1 onion
1 tablespoon cooking oil
½ green pepper
½ red pepper
8 oz / 250 g tomatoes or 1 (8-oz / 227-g) can
½ clove of garlic
Salt and freshly ground pepper
A sprinkling of chopped basil
4 large eggs
2 rashers streaky bacon
A fairly deep 1½-pint / 900-ml ovenproof dish

Peel and finely slice the onion. Warm the oil in a frying pan, add the onion and cook it over a gentle heat to soften without colouring. Meanwhile, take the seeds out of the peppers and slice the flesh into neat strips. Peel the tomatoes; to do this cover them with boiling water, count 20, pour off the water and replace it with cold. The tomatoes should now peel easily. Cut them in quarters, chop them roughly, add them to the cooking onion and cook them gently to evaporate the moisture.

Add the sliced pepper and cook it for about 10 minutes to soften it slightly.

Peel the outer skin off the half-clove of garlic then slice the garlic, sprinkle it with salt, crush it to a cream under the blade of a heavy knife and add it to the mixture with salt and freshly ground pepper to season and a sprinkling of chopped basil. Turn the mixture into the dish.

Break the eggs into a basin and beat them well together. Season with salt and pepper and pour them on to the vegetables. Cut the bacon rashers in half and stretch them on a board under the blade of a heavy knife to elongate them. Then lay them on top of the egg, overlapping the sides of the dish by about ½ inch / 1 cm; this will also help to prevent them from shrinking.

Bake the Piperade in a moderate oven, *Gas Mark 4 or 350 degrees F or 180 degrees C*, for about 25 minutes. The egg should be set. You may need to put the dish under the grill to crisp the bacon.

Note: This is a good dish to put together early in the day ready for baking. If the base mixture is completely cold it may take a little longer for the egg to set.

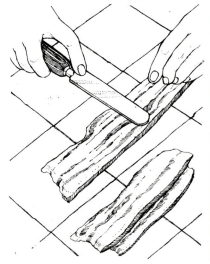

Onion and Egg Gougère

The ring of choux pastry is baked with the filling

For 4 people

FOR THE CHOUX PASTRY
  CIRCLE
4 tablespoons cooking oil
¼ pint / 150 ml water
3 oz / 75 g plain flour
A good pinch of salt
2 eggs
Greaseproof paper
FOR THE FILLING
2 oz / 50 g Cheddar cheese
6 eggs
½ pint / 300 ml milk
A bouquet garni
4 oz / 125 g button mushrooms
1 bunch spring onions
1 oz / 25 g butter
1 oz / 25 g flour
Salt and freshly ground black pepper

Put the oil and water into a medium-sized pan and bring them to the boil. Meanwhile, sift the flour on to a piece of greaseproof paper, adding a pinch of salt. As soon as the liquid has come to the boil, take it off the heat, let the bubbles subside, then add the flour and immediately beat sharply with a wooden spoon or a spatula to blend the flour smoothly into the mixture. This should leave the sides of the pan cleanly.

Break 1 of the eggs into the mixture (there is no need to cool it), and beat well. Add the other egg in the same way; the mixture should be smooth and shiny and is now ready to use.

Cut the cheese into small cubes and stir into the choux pastry. Lightly grease an oven-proof dish and carefully line the edge of the dish with the choux pastry mixture.

Hardboil the eggs then run cold water over them and shell them. Cut the eggs in half lengthwise, keeping back 1 yolk, and arrange the rest inside the choux pastry surround.

Put the milk into a pan with the bouquet garni and bring it very slowly to the boil, then leave it on one side for a few minutes to infuse it with the flavour of the bouquet garni.

Wash the mushrooms and halve them, then trim the spring onions and cut them into 2-inch / 5-cm lengths. Melt the butter in a saucepan, add the mushrooms and onions and cook them gently, with a lid on the pan, for 2 minutes until they are just tender.

Sprinkle the flour over, then strain the milk into the pan and stir the sauce over a gentle heat until it comes to the boil. Season carefully with salt and freshly ground pepper. Coat the eggs with the sauce.

Cook the gougère just above the centre of a fairly hot oven, *Gas Mark 6 or 400 degrees F or 200 degrees C*, for about 40 minutes.

Just before serving, rub the reserved hardboiled egg yolk through a sieve and use to garnish the top of the gougère.

Serve the gougère with a salad, or a hot vegetable if you prefer.

Carbonara

For 2 people

4 oz/125 g streaky bacon
2 oz/50 g pasta (this can be noodles or macaroni or any of the prettily shaped pastas)
4 eggs
2 oz/50 g cheese, grated
Salt and pepper
2 tablespoons water

Cut off the bacon rinds then with a pair of scissors, cut the bacon pieces directly into a frying pan. Allow the bacon to colour slightly over a gentle heat without extra fat.

Meanwhile cook the pasta in boiling salted water for 5 to 7 minutes until it is tender, then drain.

Beat the eggs in the pan used for the pasta. Add the grated cheese, the salt and pepper, the 2 tablespoons of water and the pasta. When the bacon is cooked, pour this mixture into it and stir it gently over a moderate heat as you would an omelet. Serve from the pan when just set.

Note: You can, of course, use cooked left-over pasta for this recipe.

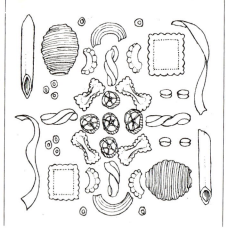

Quiche Lorraine

(Illustrated on page 75)

FOR THE PASTRY
6 oz/175 g plain flour
2 pinches salt
1½ oz/40 g margarine
1½ oz/40 g lard or white fat
Cold water to mix
FOR THE FILLING
4 oz/125 g spring onions
6 oz/175 g streaky bacon
2 oz/50 g margarine
2 eggs
¼ pint/150 ml, plus 4 tablespoons milk
4 tablespoons single cream
2 oz/50 g Cheddar cheese, grated
1 9-inch/23-cm loose-based flan tin

To make the pastry Sift the flour and salt into a mixing bowl. Add the fats and cut them into small pieces, then rub them into the flour with the tips of your fingers. Mix with just enough cold water to make a firm dough.

To line a flan tin Roll the pastry into a round just over 1 inch/2.5 cm wider than the top measurement of the tin. Put the tin on to a baking tray, then lift the pastry over a rolling pin and slip it into the tin. Press the pastry into the base and up the sides of the tin, being very careful not to break the pastry.

To form a neat edge to the flan, make a ledge round the inside. Lay your left forefinger round the top edge of the flan and with the other hand press the pastry over your finger to make a ledge. With the fingers, pinch the ledge of pastry upwards to flute the top. Leave it in the refrigerator or a cool place, while making the filling.

To make the filling Trim the onions; slice the base of each one finely and cut the green tops into ½-inch/1-cm pieces. Cut the rinds from the bacon rashers with a pair of scissors, then cut the rashers into small pieces. Cook the bacon gently in a frying pan. Add the margarine and the onions and cook them gently, without browning them, for a 2 to 3 minutes.

Break the eggs into a bowl and beat them well, then beat in the milk, cream and grated cheese. Stir in the cooked mixture then season well with salt and freshly ground black pepper. Pour the mixture into the pastry case.

Bake the flan just above the centre of a fairly hot oven, *Gas Mark 6 or 400 degrees F or 200 degrees C*, for 35 minutes.

To take the flan out of the tin, stand the base on a bowl or can of a smaller diameter than the base and let the flan tin sides drop. Serve on the aluminium base. If using a flan ring on an upturned baking tray, slip the flan, in the ring, on to the serving dish then lift the ring upwards to remove it.

To freeze Slip the flan tin from the flan. When it is cold put the flan into a polythene bag, still on the base, and freeze it. The flans can be stacked when frozen. The strong base helps to protect them from being cracked or broken in the freezer. We reheat the flans from frozen in a moderately hot oven, *Gas Mark 5 or 375 degrees F or 190 degrees C*, for 20 minutes. If they are thawed first they take about half this time to heat.

Note: The egg mixture in this recipe tends to make the base of the pastry a little moist after thawing. To counteract this, if you intend to freeze the flan beat 2 teaspoons of plain flour into the egg mixture.

To make a 6-inch/15-cm flan Use 4 oz/125 g flour, 1 pinch salt, 1 oz/25 g each of margarine and lard with a filling of 2 oz/50 g each of spring onions and bacon, 1 oz/25 g margarine, 1 egg, ¼ pint/150 ml milk, 2 tablespoons single cream and 1 oz/25 g Cheddar cheese, grated.

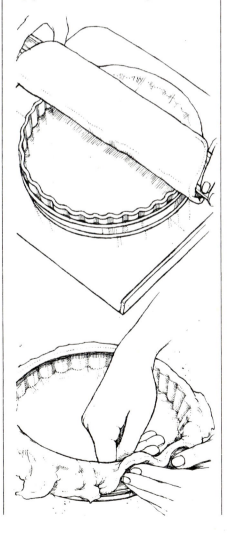

Savoury Butters, Sauces and Dressings

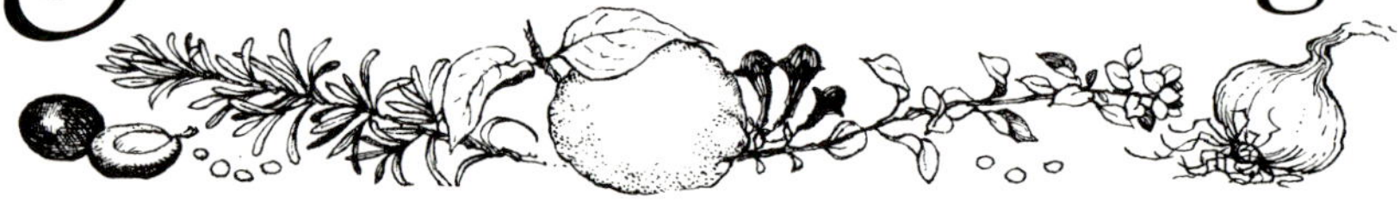

The egg-based and butter-based sauces are all good with plainly cooked dishes and vegetables.

Savoury butters are not only for using on cooked food, but make an excellent base for sandwiches; spread with anchovy butter and packed with crisp chopped lettuce, a sandwich has a little sparkle.

We make our own mayonnaise all the time in the Woman and Home kitchen, and having once mastered the blender method you will find it's easy to make. Béchamel is indispensable for using as a part of a recipe; French dressing is useful for innumerable salads.

Savoury Butters

All these butters should be served chilled, and spoonfuls scooped out on to the hot meat. They store well in the refrigerator, covered with foil.

Maître-d'Hôtel Butter

Serve on top of grilled steak, chops or grilled gammon. Also on creamed potatoes, butter or haricot beans and all grilled white fish.

Makes about 4 oz/125 g
4 oz/125 g butter, softened
2 level tablespoons chopped
 parsley
A little lemon juice
A pinch of cayenne pepper

Beat all ingredients together. Pack into a small earthenware pot and smooth the top.

Hungarian Butter

Serve with grilled or fried steak; lamb, pork or veal chops. Excellent with grilled liver.

Makes about 4 oz/125 g
4 oz/125 g butter, softened
2 gherkins, chopped
3 olives, stuffed or pitted, chopped
6 capers, chopped

Beat all ingredients together and pack into a small pot.

Anchovy Butter

Serve with grilled or fried steak, lamb cutlets or veal.

Makes about 4 oz/125 g
4 oz/125 g butter, softened
10 anchovy fillets, chopped

Beat all ingredients together, then pack into a small pot.

The three following butters are special favourites to spread between sliced French bread and serve hot. We have used them all at one meal – one loaf of each to accompany a salad main course. We lined the basket for the mustard bread with a deep yellow napkin, the herb bread with a green napkin and the garlic with white, and the guests quickly got the message.

For one long French loaf 4 oz / 125 g butter is enough.

Mustard Butter

Beat enough of your favourite mustard into softened butter.

Herb Butter

Beat 2 level tablespoons of chopped, mixed herbs into the softened butter and season well with salt and freshly ground pepper. Parsley, marjoram, thyme and a little chopped mint or chives give a good mix.

Garlic Butter

Beat 1 or 2 crushed cloves of garlic into the softened butter. Season to taste with salt and freshly ground pepper.

Sauces

Béchamel Sauce

Makes 1 pint / 600 ml
1 pint / 600 ml milk
A bouquet garni
A blade of mace
6 black peppercorns
2 oz / 50 g margarine
2 oz / 50 g plain flour
Salt and pepper

Put the milk into a pan with the bouquet garni, mace and peppercorns. Bring the milk very slowly to the boil then draw it off the heat and leave it for a few minutes to infuse the flavour of the herbs. Strain it to remove herbs and rinse the pan.

Melt the margarine in the pan, take it off the heat and stir in the flour. Using a small whisk, beat in the herb-flavoured milk, take it off the heat and, when it is quite smooth, return it to the heat and stir the sauce until it thickens and boils thoroughly. Add salt and pepper to taste.

White Sauce

Makes ¾ pint/450 ml
1 oz/25 g butter
1 oz/25 g plain flour
¾ pint/450 ml milk
Salt and freshly ground white pepper

Melt the butter in a saucepan, take it off the heat and stir in the flour then the milk. Stir the sauce over a low heat, increasing it slightly when the sauce is smooth. Bring the sauce to the boil, simmer for 1 minute then season with salt and pepper.

Hollandaise Sauce

(Blender method)

Serve with salmon or trout, grilled, poached or baked white fish, asparagus, broccoli spears or baby new potatoes.

Makes about ½ pint/300 ml
3 tablespoons wine or cider vinegar
12 peppercorns
1 bay leaf
2 blades of mace
8 oz/250 g butter, softened
4 egg yolks
Salt and pepper if necessary

Put the vinegar into a pan with the peppercorns, bay leaf and mace. Boil them together until the vinegar is reduced by half, then leave it on one side to infuse the flavours.
    Melt the butter over a low heat. Put the egg yolks into a blender goblet. Strain the vinegar on to the eggs. Put the lid on and switch on for a second. Add the hot butter through the hole in the lid.

Hollandaise as a dip This is particularly enjoyable with small new potatoes cooked in their skins. With baked jacket potatoes it makes a substantial snack.

Buttered Egg Sauce

Excellent with grilled, poached, baked or steamed cod, haddock, halibut or turbot.

Makes about ½ pint/300 ml
3 hardboiled eggs
6 oz/175 g butter
2 heaped tablespoons chopped parsley
Salt
A little lemon juice
A pinch of cayenne pepper

Shell the hardboiled eggs and chop them finely. Melt the butter gently and stir in the chopped hardboiled egg and the parsley. Season the sauce with salt, and sharpen it with lemon juice and cayenne pepper.

Whipped Butter Sauce

(Blender method)

Serve with boiled or baked white fish, asparagus or boiled chicken.

Makes 4 oz/125 g
4 oz/125 g butter, softened
4 tablespoons warm water

Put the well-softened butter into the blender goblet, switch on and gradually add the warm water. Turn off and scrape down the side of the goblet as necessary.

Dressings

French Dressing

If you have a family to feed, make a good quantity of this dressing, as it keeps well for months. Use a wide-necked jar with a plastic lid and remember to shake the bottle before use.

Makes about 1¾ pints/1 litre
½ pint/300 ml wine vinegar
1¼ pints/750 ml cooking oil
4 level teaspoons caster sugar
2 level teaspoons salt
½ level teaspoon freshly ground
  black pepper
2 level teaspoons French mustard

Put all the ingredients into the jar, cover it and shake well.
Note: To add garlic flavour to a salad, cut a clove in half and rub it round the salad bowl, just to give a hint of flavour.

Mayonnaise

Home-made mayonnaise is very easy to make in a blender and we give this method first; this amount makes about 1 pint/ 600 ml. It keeps well in a screw-topped jar or plastic container in the refrigerator.

Makes 1 pint/600 ml
2 eggs (these should be at room
  temperature)
3 level teaspoons French mustard
A good pinch of caster sugar
Salt and freshly ground white
  pepper
About 2 tablespoons vinegar, cider
  vinegar or lemon juice
¾ pint/450 ml cooking oil

Break the eggs into the blender goblet. Add the mustard, sugar, salt, pepper and vinegar or lemon juice and blend together for a second. With the blender still switched on, pour in the oil very slowly at first, then in a steady stream. The mixture will thicken; it is easy to tell when this is happening as the noise of the blender changes. After this add the oil a little more quickly. Season the mayonnaise, put it into plastic covered containers and store in the refrigerator.

When you are using the mayonnaise to accompany or coat salads, beat a little hot water into it to lighten and thin it slightly.

Making mayonnaise by hand
Use only the egg yolks, putting them into a bowl with the French mustard, sugar, salt and pepper. Very gradually beat in the oil, drop by drop, until the mixture starts to thicken, then add it a little more quickly. Add the vinegar or lemon juice, a few drops at a time, to thin the mixture and keep it the right consistency.

Variations

Curry Mayonnaise To serve with hardboiled eggs or cold chicken; add curry paste to taste.

Apricot Mayonnaise Good with cold ham or cold salt beef. Add ¼ pint/150 ml natural yoghurt or soured cream to the mayonnaise. Sieve 8 oz/250 g fresh or dried stewed apricots and add to the mayonnaise. Two tablespoons of sieved apricot jam can be used instead.

Prawn Cocktail Mayonnaise
Add a few drops of Tabasco sauce to the mayonnaise with 1 level tablespoon of tomato purée, 2 teaspoons of sherry and salt and pepper.

Use to coat prawns or other seafood.

Green Goddess Dressing

This can be served with any green salad, but it is especially good with a shredded cabbage salad, with a fish salad, or with globe artichokes.

Makes just over ¾ pint/450 ml
6 spring onions
4 anchovies
¼ pint/150 ml mayonnaise
¼ pint/150 ml soured cream
¼ pint/150 ml natural yoghurt or
  buttermilk
4 level tablespoons finely chopped
  parsley
1 teaspoon lemon juice
2 teaspoons tarragon vinegar
Salt and freshly ground pepper

Chop the onion tops (green parts only) with the anchovies, mixing them well together.

Beat in the remaining ingredients, and season carefully. Alternatively chop the onions roughly with the anchovies, put all the ingredients into the blender and switch on for 2 to 3 seconds, not long enough to blend the mixture completely.

To make an unusual potato salad Scrub new potatoes, cook them in their skins, halve or slice them and coat them with Green Goddess Dressing, while

they are still hot. Garnish with chopped anchovies.

Quick Yoghurt Dressing

Makes about ¼ pint/150 ml
¼ pint/150 ml soured cream or
  natural yoghurt
2 tablespoons cider vinegar
1 level teaspoon French mustard
A good pinch of caster sugar
Salt and freshly ground pepper
A few drops of Worcester sauce

Mix all the ingredients together thoroughly.
Note: 2 tablespoons of tomato ketchup added to this dressing makes an excellent prawn cocktail dressing.

Coleslaw Dressing

This is a useful dressing for a potato salad or for hardboiled eggs. It keeps well for several weeks in a screw-topped glass jar or covered plastic container in the refrigerator.

Makes about ¾ pint/450 ml
2 level tablespoons flour
½ level teaspoon salt
1 level teaspoon dry mustard
3 level teaspoons caster sugar
A good pinch of cayenne pepper
2 oz/50 g butter
½ pint/300 ml milk
2 eggs, beaten
¼ pint/150 ml cider vinegar
A little single cream or top milk

Sieve the flour, salt, dry mustard, caster sugar and cayenne pepper.

Melt the butter, take it off the heat and stir in the dry ingredients. Add the milk, beaten eggs and vinegar. Whisk the mixture over a gentle heat with a small whisk until it comes to the boil and thickens, then simmer it for a few moments. Pour the mixture into a screw-topped glass jar or plastic container, cover tightly and store in the refrigerator.

Note: When you are using the dressing take out the amount you need and beat it very well, then add a little single cream or top milk to thin the dressing and mellow the flavour. We suggest serving the dressing in a separate dish. Use it to coat the cabbage or any of the following mixtures lightly:

Shredded cabbage and grated carrot

Shredded cabbage and chopped parsley

Shredded cabbage, peanuts and raisins

Shredded red cabbage and sliced green apples

Caraway seeds or crushed coriander seeds make an unusual addition to any of the above.

Variations

Tomato Dressing Add 2 tablespoons tomato ketchup. This is a good dressing for prawn cocktail or over skinned and sliced tomatoes sprinkled with chopped chives.

Yoghurt Dressing Add 4 tablespoons natural yoghurt. This is milder than mayonnaise for a potato salad. Sprinkle with fresh chopped mint.

Blue Cheese Dressing Add 1 oz/25 g sieved blue cheese; you may find it easier to blend the dressing and cheese in the blender. This dressing is unusual in a rice salad; it is also particularly good with a crunchy celery and apple salad.

Chiffonade Dressing

This is one of the best dressings for a rice salad. Add any selection of salad vegetables or cooked vegetables to cold boiled rice and moisten the mixture with the dressing.

French or runner beans, cooked and allowed to get cold, make a good first course coated with this dressing. For an unusual salad, add this dressing to raw chopped spinach.

Makes just over $\frac{1}{4}$ pint / 150 ml
2 teaspoons green pepper, chopped
4 teaspoons red pepper, chopped
$\frac{1}{4}$ pint / 150 ml French dressing
  (see page 67)
$\frac{1}{2}$ level teaspoon chopped chives
1 hardboiled egg
A good pinch of paprika pepper
Salt and freshly ground black
  pepper

Mix the red and green chopped pepper into the French dressing, and add the chives. Chop the hardboiled egg finely and add it to the dressing with the paprika and salt and freshly ground pepper.

Vegetables and Salads

This chapter includes an exciting variety of main courses, some light and some hearty, besides interesting ways with vegetables to accompany a main course. Careful cooking is the watchword where all vegetables are concerned.

Never overcook green vegetables, as quite apart from spoiling the flavour, texture, colour and food value, they are reduced in quantity and so far more are required.

For root vegetables use a potato peeler where you can – it is so much more economical – but young vegetables, such as new potatoes and carrots, need only be scrubbed. Cut vegetables to even-sized pieces to ensure the same cooking time.

To brighten the colour of crisply cooked green vegetables, rinse them with a splash of cold water while they are still in the colander, and reheat with a knob of butter.

Before incorporating it in the soup or gravy use the water from the vegetables to heat the vegetable dish.

Vegetables are also very versatile as salad ingredients. Even a few crisp lettuce leaves, partnered with one of our dressings that may be new to you, can make a welcome change. The growing fashion of serving a simple salad with a hot main course, as well as or instead of a hot vegetable, is one we really enjoy.

Creamed Potatoes

Well beaten, really smooth and carefully seasoned creamed potatoes are a joy to eat. The secret is adding hot milk and butter.

For 5 or 6 people
3 lb / 1.5 kg potatoes, peeled
¼ pint / 150 ml milk
2 oz / 25 g butter
Salt and freshly ground black
pepper

Boil the potatoes until they are tender. Put them through a Mouli vegetable mill or beat them with a potato masher to make them completely smooth.

Put the milk and butter into a pan, heat them together until the butter has melted, then beat into the potato. Season well with salt and freshly ground pepper.

Boiled Rice

Allow 1½ oz/40 g long-grain rice per person

Put the rice into plenty of boiling salted water and boil it uncovered for 12 to 14 minutes. Test a grain between the fingers (when it is ready it should almost rub away), drain the rice and pour boiling water through it to separate the grains. After rinsing it will keep warm easily as excess starch will have been removed.

To prepare in advance Put the well-rinsed boiled rice in a roasting tin, cover with foil and heat in the oven.

Crispy Cabbage

For 6 people
1 green-hearted cabbage; a medium firm one is best
1 oz/25 g butter
Salt and freshly ground black pepper
A pinch of grated nutmeg (optional)

Cut off any discoloured leaves, then wash and quarter the cabbage and shred finely with a sharp knife on a wooden board; alternatively, coarsely shred in an electric shredder.
Put the shredded cabbage into a large pan and add a good pinch of salt and enough boiling water just to cover the cabbage. Boil it quickly for about 5 minutes, tossing it round with a fork so that it cooks evenly. Drain the cabbage, then melt the butter in the same pan; replace the cabbage and toss it for 1 to 2 minutes. Add salt and freshly ground pepper to taste, and grated nutmeg, if liked.
Note: A medium-sized white cabbage can be used; a good teaspoon of chopped parsley, tossed in with the butter, gives it a nice bright colour.

Spring Onions with Peas

This combination is very good, especially as an accompaniment to fried liver and bacon, sausages or a boiled bacon joint.

For 5 or 6 people
1 bunch spring onions
1 lb/500 g frozen peas
1 pint/600 ml water
Salt, pepper and a pinch of sugar
A little beurre manié

Trim the onions and cut them in half. Bring the water to the boil, put in the peas, onions, salt, pepper and sugar. Cook gently for about 7 minutes. Stirring all the time, add a few dots of beurre manié to thicken to the consistency you like. It should just hold the peas in suspension.

Beurre manié
This thickening is used in French cookery a great deal. It is very quick to use and convenient to add, for as the butter melts, the flour is stirred smoothly into the liquid.
Put 2 oz/50 g of butter on to a plate and soften it by beating it with a palette knife. Gradually beat in 1½ oz/40 g flour. Keep the paste ready to thicken soups, stews or sauces.

Buttered Beetroot

To serve with cold meats and baked potatoes.

For 4 people
1 lb/500 g cooked beetroot
1 clove garlic
2 oz/50 g butter
Salt and freshly ground black
  pepper

Peel the beetroot and grate it coarsely. Crush the garlic, melt the butter in a pan and add the garlic. Cook gently for 1 to 2 minutes then add the beetroot. Toss over a gentle heat until it is heated through, then season well with salt and black pepper if needed.

Glazed Parsnips or Carrots

Especially good with beef or pork dishes.

For 4 people
1 lb/500 g parsnips or carrots
1 oz/25 g butter
1 oz/25 g brown sugar
2 teaspoons lemon juice
6 teaspoons dry cider
A large pinch of salt
Freshly ground black pepper

Peel the vegetables with a potato peeler then cut them into 2-inch/5-cm sticks. Plunge these into boiling salted water, and cook for about 7 minutes until just tender. Drain them well and turn them into an ovenproof dish. Melt the butter and mix it with the brown sugar, lemon juice, dry cider, salt and freshly ground black pepper. Pour this mixture over the carrots or parsnips and bake them in a hot oven, at *Gas Mark 6 or 400 degrees F or 200 degrees C*, for 20 minutes or until the vegetables are a golden brown.

Spinach Loaf

This makes a good hot or cold main course with rolls and butter, or half slices can be served as a party first course.

For 5 or 6 people
2 large packets of chopped frozen
  spinach, thawed
2 eggs
¼ pint/150 ml single cream
4 oz/125 g cheese, grated
Salt, freshly ground black pepper
  and grated nutmeg
A 1-lb/500-g loaf tin
A little cooking oil
Greaseproof paper

Brush the inside of the loaf tin with a little cooking oil.
  Drain any liquid off the thawed spinach. Beat the eggs, then add the cream and grated cheese. Mix in the raw spinach. Season the mixture with freshly ground black pepper, salt and a sprinkling of grated nutmeg. Pour it into the tin and cover the top loosely with a piece of greaseproof paper.
  Stand the loaf tin in a roasting pan and pour hot water round it to come halfway up the loaf tin. Bake the loaf in a moderate oven, *about Gas Mark 4 or 350 degrees F or 180 degrees C*, for 1 hour, then loosen it carefully round the edges and turn it on to a board for slicing. If serving

cold, leave to cool in the tin before turning out and slicing.

Note: 2 lb/1 kg fresh spinach may be used; wash the leaves well and boil for 2 to 3 minutes, drain well and chop.

Asparagus Soufflé Flan

For 4 to 5 people
FOR THE FLAN CASE
6 oz/175 g plain flour
A pinch of salt
1½ oz/40 g butter
1½ oz/40 g lard
About 3 tablespoons milk
A flan tin 9 inches/23 cm in diameter
FOR THE FILLING
1 (14-oz/400-g) can asparagus or cut asparagus spears
1½ oz/40 g butter
1½ oz/40 g plain flour
½ pint/300 ml milk
4 oz/125 g Cheddar cheese, grated
2 eggs
Salt and pepper

Sift the flour and salt into a mixing bowl, add the fats and cut them into small pieces then rub them into the flour with the tips of your fingers. When the mixture looks like breadcrumbs add just enough milk to make a firm dough.

Line flan ring with pastry (see page 62).

Drain the asparagus and arrange in a wheel shape round the base of the flan so that when it is cut, each slice will have the same amount of asparagus. Leave it in a cool place while making the soufflé mixture.

Melt the butter in a saucepan,

take it off the heat and stir in the flour, then the milk. Stir the sauce over a low heat, increasing it slightly when the sauce is smooth. Bring the sauce to the boil, simmer for 1 minute. Take the pan off the heat and beat in the grated cheese. Beat in the eggs, one at a time. Season the sauce with salt and pepper and pour it into the flan.

Bake the flan in a moderately hot oven, about *Gas Mark 6 or 400 degrees F or 200 degrees C,* for 30 to 40 minutes, until the soufflé has risen above the pastry.

Although the hot flan should be eaten at once before the centre falls flat, it is very good cold and is useful for packed lunches and picnics.

Note: Fresh asparagus, cooked, is of course ideal. Alternatively, use halved cooked leeks.

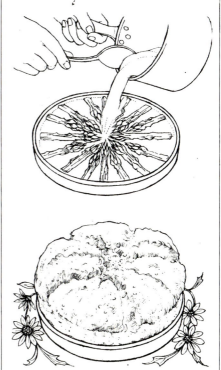

Bean Hot Pot

For 5 to 6 hungry people
*12 oz/375 g soya, kidney, haricot
or brown beans
1 lb/500 g stewing beef or lamb
2 tablespoons melted dripping or oil
3 medium-sized onions, peeled and
sliced
1 (14-oz/396-g) can tomatoes
2 tablespoons tomato purée
¼ level teaspoon dried basil
¾ pint/450 ml stock or water
Salt and freshly ground black
pepper
A 4-pint/2.25-litre casserole*

Cover the beans with cold water
and leave them to soak overnight then drain them and boil
in fresh, unsalted water for 30
minutes, making sure there is
always sufficient water to cover
them. Salt is not added to the
beans while they are cooking as
it toughens the skins and in-
creases the cooking time.
    Cut the meat into 1-inch/
2.5-cm cubes. Heat the dripping
or oil in a pan and fry the meat,
a few pieces at a time, until it is
well browned all over. As the
meat is browned, transfer it to
the casserole; then fry the onions
in the remaining dripping. Add
the tomatoes (and their juice),
the tomato purée, basil, stock or
water to the onions, and bring
to the boil.
    Drain the beans and add them
to the sauce, then pour the mixture over the meat. Stir well, and
season only with pepper. Cover
the casserole tightly and cook in
a fairly slow oven, *Gas Mark 3 or
325 degrees F or 160 degrees C*, for
2 to 2 hours 30 minutes, until the
meat and beans are tender.
    Season well and serve straight
from the casserole.

Cauliflower with Cream and Herb Sauce

A supper dish.

For 4 people
*1 large cauliflower
Salt
¼ pint/150 ml single cream
1 small can pâté with herbs*

Remove the coarse outside leaves
of the cauliflower, leaving the
tender ones round the sides, and
wash it well. Half-fill a large
pan with water, salt it well and
bring it to the boil. Put in the
cauliflower, stalk downwards,
and cover the pan with a lid so
that the cauliflower cooks in the
steam. Cook the cauliflower until
it is just tender when tested with
a knife then drain well and
transfer it to a hot dish.
    Mix the cream and pâté to-
gether and heat gently in a small
pan. Pour this sauce over the
cauliflower and sprinkle the top
with paprika.
Note: A slice of lemon in the
water helps to keep the cauliflower white.

Quiche Lorraine (see page 62)

74

Stuffed Marrow Rings

For 5 people

1 medium-sized young marrow
10 oz / 300 g cooked bacon (we used up a cooked, boned bacon forehock)
1 oz / 25 g butter
4 oz / 125 g onions, finely chopped
4 oz / 125 g mushrooms, washed and chopped but not peeled
2 oz / 50 g fresh white breadcrumbs
Freshly ground black pepper
4 oz / 125 g cheese, grated
1 pint / 600 ml béchamel sauce (see page 65)

Cut the ends from the marrow, peel and reserve. Cut the marrow into slices about 1½ inches / 4 cm wide. Cut out the centre from each piece with a sharp knife, then thinly peel the skin; (this is much easier than peeling the marrow first). Plunge the marrow rings including the end pieces, into plenty of boiling salted water; bring back to the boil and boil the marrow for 5 minutes. Drain carefully in a colander, then transfer to absorbent kitchen paper and drain thoroughly. Arrange 5 rings in an ovenproof dish.

Meanwhile, mince the bacon. Melt the butter in a frying pan, add the onion and fry gently until it is tender. Add the mushrooms and fry them with the onions for a few seconds then add them to the minced bacon with 1 oz / 25 g of the breadcrumbs. Season with freshly ground pepper: extra salt will probably not be needed because of the bacon. Pile the mixture into the rings. Cut the end pieces of marrow into strips and cross the top of each ring with a piece of this marrow, divided evenly.

Beat three-quarters of the grated cheese into the béchamel sauce and use to coat the marrow rings. Mix the rest of the cheese with the remaining breadcrumbs and sprinkle over the surface. Place in a moderately hot oven, about *Gas Mark 6 or 400 degrees F or 200 degrees C*, for about 20 minutes until the marrow stuffing is hot and the top is nicely browned.

Apple Maraschino (see page 91)

Noma Roma
(Aubergine Cheese Custard)

For 3 people
2 aubergines (about 1 lb/500 g)
Salt
1 oz/25 g plain flour
Freshly ground black pepper
About 4 tablespoons cooking oil
2 eggs
¼ pint/150 ml single cream
¼ pint/150 ml milk
1 (9-oz/275-g) can tomato spaghetti sauce
2 level tablespoons Parmesan cheese, grated
1 oz/25 g fresh white breadcrumbs
A 2½-pint/1.4-litre ovenproof dish

Cut the aubergines in slices about ½ inch/1 cm thick, sprinkle them liberally with salt and leave for 30 minutes to extract the liquid. Rinse and dry.

Put the flour and a good sprinkling of pepper into a polythene bag with a little more salt. Add a few slices of aubergine at a time to the bag and shake gently in the mixture to coat the slices well. Heat the oil in a large frying pan and fry the aubergine briskly on both sides until golden, then drain on kitchen paper.

Put the slices in the base of the ovenproof dish. Beat the eggs, cream and milk together, then season and pour the mixture over the aubergine. Bake in a very moderate oven, about *Gas Mark 3 or 325 degrees F or 160 degrees C*, for 30 to 40 minutes until the eggs are just set. Heat the canned spaghetti sauce and pour this over. Mix the Parmesan cheese and breadcrumbs together and sprinkle over the top. Brown quickly under a moderate grill.

Baked Potato and Parmesan Pie

A main course

For 4 or 5 people
1 oz/25 g margarine
1 lb/500 g onions, peeled and thinly sliced
½ pint/300 ml single cream
Salt and freshly ground black pepper
2 lb/1 kg potatoes, peeled and thinly sliced
1 oz/25 g Parmesan cheese, grated
1 can anchovies
1 bayleaf
1 sprig of rosemary
1 oz/25 g butter
A little chopped parsley
A 2½-pint/1.4-litre ovenproof dish

Melt the margarine in a large pan, add the sliced onions and stir them over a gentle heat for 2 to 3 minutes. Stir in the cream and season the mixture with salt and freshly ground black pepper. Reserve a few sliced potatoes for the top and stir the remainder into the cream. Heat the mixture slowly. When it has warmed through take it off the heat and stir in the cheese.

Put half the mixture into the ovenproof dish, cover with the anchovy fillets, sprinkle the oil from the can over and add the bayleaf and rosemary. Top with the rest of the mixture. Cover with the potato slices. Melt the butter and brush half of it over the top of the potatoes. Bake in a moderate oven, about *Gas Mark 4 or 350 degrees F or 180 degrees C*, for about 1 hour. Brush the top with the rest of the butter and sprinkle with a little chopped parsley.

Pommes Boulangères

For 4 people

1 lb/500 g potatoes, weighed after peeling
2 oz/50 g butter
1 onion, diced
8 oz/250 g Cheddar cheese, grated
1 pint/600 ml béchamel sauce (see page 65)
Salt
Freshly ground black pepper

Cut the potatoes into thin slices; use an electric slicer if you have one, or a large knife. Put the slices into cold water to prevent them from discolouring.

Put the butter into an ovenproof dish and melt it in a moderate oven, about *Gas Mark 4 or 350 degrees F or 180 degrees C*, when it is melted add the diced onion and return it to the oven.

Drain the sliced potatoes and dry them on a clean tea towel or absorbent kitchen paper. Add three quarters of the cheese to the hot sauce and beat well. Add all the potatoes and stir them over a gentle heat until they are heated in the sauce. Season them with salt and freshly ground black pepper.

Take the dish out of the oven and pour the potato mixture into it. The hot dish and potatoes already heated in the sauce help to start the cooking quickly. Sprinkle the rest of the cheese on top.

Cook the potatoes just above the centre of a moderate oven, *Gas Mark 4 or 350 degrees F or 180 degrees C*, for about 1 hour and a quarter, or until the potatoes are tender; the time will

depend upon the thickness of the raw potato. Put the dish under a hot grill to brown for a few seconds if necessary, and serve large helpings on hot plates.

Baked Savoury Rice

For 6 people

2 packets frozen Savoury Vegetable Rice (sweetcorn and peppers)
2 egg yolks
¼ pint/150 ml milk
4 oz/125 g strong Cheddar cheese
Salt and freshly ground black pepper
A 2-pint/1.15-litre oval ovenproof dish

Cook the rice as directed on the packet, using ¾ pint/450 ml of water. Beat the egg yolks with the milk. Grate the cheese and add it to the yolks and milk with the cooked rice. Season with salt and freshly ground black pepper. Brush the ovenproof dish with a little melted fat and turn the mixture into it. Bake at *Gas Mark 4 or 350 degrees F or 180 degrees C*, for about 25 minutes until the mixture is set.

Cut into portions and serve, hot or cold, with a green salad and sliced tomatoes.

Lemon Potato Salad

For 6 to 8 people

3 lb / 1.5 kg new potatoes
Salt
2 or 3 sprigs of mint
The juice of 2 lemons
4 oz / 125 g butter
1 bunch of spring onions

Scrape the new potatoes and put them into boiling salted water with the sprigs of mint. Boil them for about 7 minutes (they should still be quite firm) then drain them and cut the larger ones in half, leaving the smaller ones whole.

Heat the lemon juice and melt the butter in a large frying pan, add the potatoes and cook them gently, turning them frequently until they are lightly browned. Leave to cool and when the potatoes are cold, arrange them on a serving dish.

Remove any coarse, discoloured leaves from the spring onions, snip small slices with a pair of scissors and arrange them over the dish of potatoes. If you are serving two salads on the same dish the onions make a good dividing line.

Note: If you like the skins, the potatoes need only be scrubbed.

Beetroot and Orange Salad

For 4 people

2 lb / 1 kg boiled beetroot
5 or 6 small oranges
2 tablespoons French dressing
*   (see page 67)*

Peel the beetroot and grate it coarsely or put it through an electric shredder. Grate the rind from 2 of the oranges, mix it with the French dressing and toss it into the beetroot.

Using a sharp knife cut the white pith, spirally, off the remaining oranges and slice them. Arrange these slices round the edge of the bowl, then pile the beetroot in the centre.

Tomato Salad with Dill Dressing

Can be served as a first course

For 6 people

2 lb / 1 kg ripe tomatoes, peeled
1 level teaspoon dill or dried dill
*   weed*
4 tablespoons French dressing
*   (see page 67)*

Slice the tomatoes evenly, using a sharp knife, and arrange them in a shallow dish, putting the ends and any uneven pieces below a layer of neat ones. Mix the dill or dried dill weed into the dressing and spoon it over the tomatoes.

Cucumber and Mint Salad

For 5 or 6 people
1 cucumber
2 tablespoons French dressing
(see page 67)
Mint sprigs

Slice the cucumber and lay the slices in a shallow dish. Sprinkle the French dressing over them and garnish the dish with sprigs of mint.

Four-Bean Salad

For 6 people
2 oz/50 g each of 3 or 4 of the following brightly coloured beans such as red kidney beans, butter beans, flageolets, brown borlotti beans, black-eyed beans, soya beans and, if you have them, some sprouted beans
FOR THE DRESSING
4 tablespoons oil
1 tablespoon vinegar
Salt and freshly ground pepper
A pinch of cayenne pepper
2 tablespoons freshly chopped parsley or spring onions or chives

Soak the dry beans in plenty of cold water overnight, then drain and rinse them and put them into a large pan and cover with fresh, unsalted water. Bring them very slowly to the boil and simmer gently for 1 hour 30 minutes, or until the beans are just tender. Drain all the beans and put them into a bowl.

While the beans are still hot, add the ingredients for the dressing except the parsley or spring onions or chives, and mix well.

Hot beans will absorb the dress-more easily.

Leave the beans to cool in the dressing, then add the parsley or spring onions or chives and the sprouted beans. Chill the salad before serving.
Note: A can of flaked tuna fish can be added to make a main course if you like.

Cheese Pasta Salad

For 4 or 5 people
4 oz/125 g macaroni bows or any other pasta shapes
3 sticks celery or 2 heads chicory or 6 oz/175 g white cabbage, shredded
3 small tomatoes
4 oz/125 g mushrooms
8 oz/250 g Cheddar cheese
2 tablespoons cooking oil
1 tablespoon vinegar
Salt and freshly ground black pepper

Cook the macaroni shapes in boiling salted water for about 9 minutes, just until they are tender. Drain them through a colander then rinse them with cold water; this cools the macaroni so that it can be used immediately.

Chop the celery, chicory or cabbage and add it to the macaroni. Cut the tomatoes in quarters. Wash the mushrooms and slice them. Cut the cheese into $\frac{1}{2}$-inch/1-cm cubes. Mix all these lightly with the macaroni.

Add the oil, vinegar and a good sprinkling of salt and freshly ground pepper to the salad and toss all the ingredients together with two wooden spoons.

Hot and Cold Puddings

From our hot and warming Pineapple Pudding (see page 82) to cool and delicious Yoghurt Pudding, there is a certain feeling of achievement in producing a good pudding.

A pudding more than rounds off a meal, while a hearty one can satisfy the family and therefore show economy over the complete meal provided the main course is carefully chosen.

I am often surprised by the number of men who settle for Baked Rice Pudding when a choice is offered. Maybe they are the meat and two vegetable brigade and know how good simple food can be.

Also here are puddings for dinner parties – such a visually important part of the menu. To select these from our many mouth watering recipes, has been agony for us all!

Pineapple Pudding

(Illustrated on the back jacket)

For 6 people

3 oz/75 g butter, softened
3 oz/75 g soft brown sugar
1 (1-lb/500-g) can pineapple rings
4 glacé cherries
4 oz/125 g margarine, softened
4 oz/125 g caster sugar
2 eggs
6 oz/175 g self-raising flour
Pinch of salt
1 oz/25 g desiccated coconut
4 tablespoons milk
A 2-pint/1.15-litre pudding basin
FOR THE GLAZE
The juice from the canned
*   pineapple (about ¼ pint/150 ml)*
2 level teaspoons arrowroot

Beat the softened butter and brown sugar in the basin in which the pudding is going to be cooked, then spread the mixture evenly round to coat the inside of the basin. Drain the juice from the pineapple and reserve. Put a pineapple ring in the bottom of the basin and arrange the other rings round the side. Put a whole glacé cherry in the centre of the base ring of pineapple and red cherry halves, cut side facing up, in remaining slices.

Beat the softened margarine, sugar, eggs, flour, salt, coconut and milk for 1 minute by hand or just under a minute in an electric mixer. Turn the mixture into the pineapple-lined basin and cover the top with a double sheet of greaseproof paper pleated down the centre to allow for rising during cooking. Tie the paper firmly with string.

Put the pudding into a pan with enough boiling water to come halfway up the side of the pudding; keep the water boiling and replace it with fresh boiling water as needed. Cook the pudding for 2 hours.

To make the glaze Make the glaze with the reserved ¼ pint/ 150 ml pineapple juice. Blend the arrowroot with a little water, stir it into the juice and bring it to the boil, stirring all the time.

Turn the pudding out on to a hot plate and pour over the glaze.

Le Far Breton

This is a pudding halfway between a custard and a batter, baked with a layer of rum-soaked raisins in the centre; it is sliced and served from the dish. This recipe was much enjoyed by readers who joined our cooking holiday in Brittany, where it is often sold by the slice.

For 6 people
3 oz/75 g seedless raisins, sultanas or stoned, dried prunes
1 tablespoon rum
3 oz/75 g plain flour
2 oz/50 g caster sugar
Pinch of salt
2 eggs
1 pint/600 ml milk
2 oz/50 g butter
A shallow 2-pint/1.15-litre earthenware dish

Put the fruit into a small basin, add the rum, cover and leave it overnight.

Sift the flour into a bowl, add the sugar, salt and eggs and mix well. Bring the milk just to the boil and pour it into the mixture, stirring well to make a smooth consistency. Cut all but ½ oz/15 g of the butter into small pieces and beat it into the batter; as this will still be hot the butter will melt.

Smear the inside of the dish with the rest of the butter, pour in half the mixture and bake the pudding in a moderately hot oven, at *Gas Mark 6 or 400 degrees F or 200 degrees C*, for 20 minutes. Remove from the oven and spread the fruit over it. Cover this with the rest of the mixture and bake for a further 25 minutes.

Because the base is firmer than the centre, as it has been baked longer, it forms a firmer edge which allows slices to be cut and lifted out neatly.

Note: If you use a deeper dish, bake the pudding a little longer.

Upside-Down Ginger Pears

For 8 people
FOR THE UPSIDE-DOWN
MIXTURE
3 oz | 75 g butter
3 oz | 75 g soft brown sugar
*1 (1-lb 13-oz | 900-g) can pear
  halves*
8 glacé cherries
FOR THE GINGER SPONGE
4 oz | 125 g golden syrup
4 oz | 125 g black treacle
4 oz | 125 g butter
3 oz | 75 g soft brown sugar
1 level tablespoon marmalade
4 oz | 125 g self-raising flour
Salt
1 level teaspoon ground ginger
1 level teaspoon mixed spice
½ level teaspoon bicarbonate of soda
4 oz | 125 g plain wholewheat flour
2 eggs
¼ pint | 150 ml milk
*A roasting tin 7½ inches | 19 cm by
  11½ inches | 29 cm across the top*

Butter the inside of the tin. Place the butter and soft brown sugar in a pan over a low heat and melt. Open the can of pears and drain the juice, then arrange them in the tin, cut side downwards, with a glacé cherry in the centre of each. Pour the melted mixture over them.

Weigh the golden syrup and black treacle into a pan; add the butter, soft brown sugar and the marmalade; melt them together over a low heat, then leave them on one side to cool while preparing the rest of the ingredients.

Sift together the self-raising flour, pinch of salt, ground ginger, mixed spice and bicarbonate of soda and stir in the wholewheat flour.

Beat the eggs together and add them to the cooled, melted ingredients with the milk; pour these into the dry ingredients and mix well. Pour this mixture over the pears (it should be a pouring consistency at this stage).

Bake in a very moderate oven, *Gas Mark 3 or 325 degrees F or 160 degrees C,* for 1½ hours. Turn the pudding out to serve.

Serve with custard or a mixture of equal quantities of cool custard and yoghurt.

Rhubarb and Raisin Roll

This is also an excellent hot pudding with apple slices and blackberries instead of rhubarb and raisins.

For 6 people
6 oz | 175 g caster sugar
1 tablespoon lemon juice
*¼ pint | 150 ml plus 4 tablespoons
  water*
8 oz | 250 g plain flour
3 level teaspoons baking powder
¼ level teaspoon salt
4 oz | 125 g margarine
1½ oz | 40 g rolled oats
About ¼ pint | 150 ml milk
*1 lb | 500 g rhubarb, washed and
  chopped into ½-inch | 1-cm
  lengths*
3 oz | 75 g brown sugar
1 level teaspoon ground cinnamon
4 oz | 125 g raisins
1 oz | 25 g margarine, melted

Put the caster sugar, lemon juice and water into a pan. Melt the sugar over a gentle heat, then bring to the boil for 2 minutes. Leave on one side to cool.

Sift the flour, baking powder and salt into a mixing bowl, then rub in the margarine with the tips of your fingers. Stir in the rolled oats, then just enough milk to form a soft, but not sticky, dough, just a little softer than for shortcrust.

Turn the dough on to a floured board and roll, not too thinly, into a rectangle. Trim the rectangle to measure about 12 inches/30 cm by 8 inches/20 cm.

Mix the rhubarb, brown sugar, cinnamon and raisins together well, then brush the rectangle with half the melted margarine. Sprinkle the fruit mixture thickly over the rectangle, then roll it up. Cut the roll into 8 even-sized slices, lift them on a fish slice and lay them cut side down in a greased fireproof dish (we use a roasting tin). Brush the surface with the remaining melted margarine. Pour round the cooled syrup and cook the pudding in a fairly hot oven, *Gas Mark 6 or 400 degrees F or 200 degrees C*, for 25 to 30 minutes.

Serve with cream or custard. *Note:* 2 sliced bananas added to the filling instead of the raisins give an unusual flavour.

Special Baked Apples

For 5 people
5 medium-sized cooking apples
*5 slices of brown bread from a
    large loaf*
5 oz/150 g sultanas
5 oz/150 g soft brown sugar
2¼ oz/65 g butter
*An ovenproof dish about 10 inches/
    25 cm in diameter*

Wipe the apples and remove the cores. Score round each apple lightly with a sharp knife. Cut each slice of bread into a circle using a 3-inch/7.5-cm round cutter. Arrange the bread in the heatproof dish and place an apple on each piece. Mix the sultanas and the brown sugar together and heap into the apple cavities. Top each one with a knob of the butter.

Bake in a moderate oven, at *Gas Mark 4 or 350 degrees F or 180 degrees C*, for about 45 minutes or until the apples are tender.

Note: The bread beneath the apples catches the juices during the cooking and makes the serving much easier.

Pancakes with Lemon

For 4 or 5 people
FOR THE PANCAKES
4 oz | 125 g plain flour
A pinch of salt
1 egg
¼ pint | 150 ml milk
¼ pint | 150 ml water
1 oz | 25 g butter
A frying or omelet pan with a base
  of 6 inches | 15 cm to 7 inches |
  18 cm in diameter
TO SERVE THE PANCAKES
The juice from about 2 lemons
Caster sugar to taste
A little melted butter
A lemon cut into 4 to 5 wedges

Sift the flour into a mixing bowl with the salt. Break the egg into the centre of the flour, then add the milk. Mixing from the centre, gradually incorporate the flour from round the side and beat the batter well, holding the wooden spoon with the rounded side upwards to incorporate air. When the batter is ready to use (it should be smooth and shiny, and small bubbles should rise to the surface) stir in the water.

Heat the frying pan then melt the butter and pour it into the batter, leaving a light coating on the base of the pan. Place the pan over a moderate heat, dip a ladle into the batter and scoop up about 2 tablespoons; this is just enough to coat the base of the pan thinly. Using a ladle makes it easier to judge the right amount of mixture each time. Pour a ladle of the batter into the pan, swirling the batter quickly round the base of the pan to coat evenly and thinly and put the pan back over a high heat for a few seconds.

To toss the pancake, loosen it round the edges with a palette knife, slip it to the edge of the pan, away from the handle, and give the pan a quick flick into the air to turn the pancake. (If your courage fails, flick the pancake over with the palette knife).

Lift out the pancake with the palette knife or turn it straight on to a clean tea towel; this keeps it moist and flexible. Make the rest of the pancakes in the same way, stacking them as they are made.

To serve the pancakes Sprinkle each pancake with lemon juice and sugar then roll it up and lay it in a buttered ovenproof dish. Brush the surface with melted butter and heat in the oven at *Gas Mark 4 or 350 degrees F or 180 degrees C,* for 10 to 15 minutes. Sprinkle with caster sugar and serve with lemon wedges.

To freeze Stack the pancakes neatly; no need to separate them with paper but take them out of the freezer the evening before they are wanted so that thawed, they will separate easily.

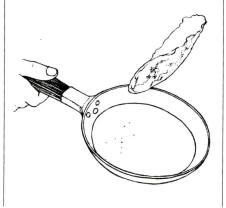

Cognac Pancakes Flambés

For 6 people
16 pancakes (opposite)
TO FLAMBÉ THE PANCAKES
4 oz / 125 g butter
2 oz / 50 g caster sugar
2 large oranges
2 tablespoons cognac

Put the butter and sugar into a large frying pan. Grate the rind finely from the oranges, squeeze the juice and add to the pan. Heat gently until the butter has melted and the sugar is dissolved.

Fold each pancake into 4 and heat them gently in the orange mixture, turning them over with tongs to heat both sides. Arrange them in an ovenproof dish and pour the remaining orange sauce over the top.

Warm the cognac slightly in a pan, pour it over the pancakes, light it with a match and bring it flaming to your guests.

Note: A miniature bottle of cognac can be used. The pancakes can be frozen with the sauce. Thaw them slowly, then heat them in a moderate oven before flaming them.

Fairlop Tart

For 4 or 5 people
FOR THE PASTRY
4 oz / 100 g plain flour
Pinch of salt
1 oz / 25 g margarine
1 oz / 25 g cooking fat
Cold water to mix
FOR THE FILLING
2 oz / 50 g fresh white breadcrumbs (these can be made quickly in a blender)
6 oz / 175 g golden syrup
The grated rind of 1 lemon
2 teaspoons lemon juice
1 egg
2 oz / 50 g sultanas
A pie plate 8½ inches / 21 cm in diameter
A small crescent-shaped cutter for the pastry decoration

Sift the flour and salt into a mixing bowl. Add the fats and cut them into small pieces, then rub them into the flour with the tips of your fingers. Mix with just enough cold water to make a firm dough. Roll it out, line the pie plate and trim the edges. Re-roll the scraps and cut out little crescents of pastry; stick these round the edge of the pastry with dabs of water.

Mix the breadcrumbs with the golden syrup. Beat in the lemon rind and juice and the egg. Stir in the sultanas and turn the mixture into the lined pastry plate. Smooth over the surface.

Bake the tart in a moderately hot oven, at *Gas Mark 5 or 375 degrees F or 190 degrees C*, for about 30 minutes. This is good hot or cold and can be served with custard.

Note: The tart freezes well, and must be thawed at room temperature for about 1 hour.

Hot Strawberry or Apricot Soufflé

For 6 people
3 individual trifle sponges or about
3 oz/75 g of sponge cake
The grated rind and juice of 1
orange
1 (15-oz/425-g) can strawberry
or apricot pie filling
2 egg whites
4 oz/125 g caster sugar
A 2-pint/1.15-litre soufflé dish

Light the oven at *Gas Mark 3 or 300 degrees F or 150 degrees C,* so that it will be ready to bake the soufflé.

Line the base of the dish with sponge (there is no need to grease it first) and sprinkle over the orange juice. Turn the strawberry fruit filling into a mixing bowl and stir in the orange rind. Whip the egg whites very stiffly then whisk in half the sugar and whisk again until the same stiff consistency is reached. Lightly fold in the rest of the sugar, then fold this mixture into the fruit and turn it immediately into the soufflé dish.

Bake the soufflé just above the centre of the slow oven for 45 minutes. Serve at once.

Ratafia Pears

For 6 people
3 egg yolks
1 oz/25 g caster sugar
2 oz/50 g plain flour
¾ pint/450 ml milk
2 oz/50 g ratafia biscuits or
macaroons
1 oz/25 g butter
3 small ripe dessert pears
3 tablespoons marmalade
A fairly shallow 1½-pint/900-ml
heat-proof dish

Put the egg yolks into a mixing bowl and beat in the caster sugar until the mixture is creamy and light in colour. Beat in the flour. Bring the milk to the boil then whisk it into the mixed ingredients. Return the mixture to the pan and bring to the boil whisking all the time to keep it smooth; it will thicken rather quickly. Take it off the heat.

Crush the biscuits with a rolling pin or in a blender and stir them into the mixture. Beat in the butter.

Butter the dish and put in the mixture. Peel the pears; cut one into quarters and remove the core, cut the other two in half and scoop out the cores with a teaspoon. Arrange the pear portions on top of the pudding. Melt the marmalade and brush it over the pears.

Bake the pudding, in a moderately hot oven, at *Gas Mark 5 or 375 degrees F or 190 degrees C,* for about 25 to 35 minutes.
Note: As an alternative topping instead of pears, put canned apricots on top of the pudding before baking and brush them with marmalade or apricot jam. Use the juice to serve with the pudding.

Mincemeat Jalousie

For 8 people

A large packet frozen puff pastry, thawed, or 1 lb/500 g puff pastry
A 14½ oz/400 g jar mincemeat
½ egg white
A little caster sugar

Lay the pastry on a floured working surface. Cut the pastry in half and roll each piece into an 8-inch/20-cm by 13-inch/33-cm rectangle.

Dampen a baking sheet and lay a piece of the rolled-out pastry on it. Spread the mincemeat evenly over the pastry to within 1 inch/2.5 cm of the edges. Brush these borders lightly with water. Fold the remaining piece of pastry in half lengthwise, top inwards, and make parallel cuts 3 inches/7.5 cm long and ½ inch/1 cm apart into the folded edge, leaving 1 inch/2.5 cm of pastry clear at each short end. Carefully unfold the pastry over the rolling pin, and use this to lift the pastry on to the base. Press the pastry edges firmly together and trim if necessary with a sharp knife. Knock up the edges neatly against your finger with the back of a knife. Beat the egg white lightly with a fork and then brush it over the pastry. Sprinkle the caster sugar over the top.

Leave the Mincemeat Jalousie in the fridge for about 30 minutes before baking at *Gas Mark 7 or 425 degrees F or 220 degrees C*, for 25 minutes until golden brown.

Lemon Haze

This pudding is the all-time favourite with readers who have come to the Woman and Home Cook School.

For 6 people

1 lemon jelly
¼ pint/150 ml water
The finely grated rind of 1 large lemon
The juice of 2 lemons
4 eggs
6 oz/175 g caster sugar
¼ pint/150 ml double cream (optional)

Cut up the jelly into individual squares, put it into a pan with the water and dissolve the jelly slowly over a low heat. Take it off the heat and stir in the grated lemon rind and juice.

Separate the whites from the yolks of the eggs. Reserve the whites and put the yolks into a large mixing bowl with the caster sugar and beat them well till they lighten in colour. Stir in the jelly. Beat the egg whites stiffly, add a tablespoon to the jelly mixture and beat it in (this prepares the mixture for the addition of the rest of the egg whites). Lightly fold the rest of the egg whites into the mixture and then pour it into a glass dish.

Decorate with swirls of whipped cream as desired.

Norwegian Cream

This is a creamy baked custard with a base of apricot jam and a topping of lightly whipped cream sprinkled with grated chocolate.

For 5 or 6 people
3 level tablespoons apricot jam
A 1½-pint/900-ml ovenproof dish
FOR THE BAKED CUSTARD
1 pint/600 ml milk
3 eggs
1 egg yolk (optional)
2 level tablespoons caster sugar
A few drops vanilla essence
Greaseproof paper
TO DECORATE
4 tablespoons double cream
3 tablespoons milk
A little grated chocolate

Spread the apricot jam over the base of the dish.

To make the baked custard
Put the milk into a pan and heat it slowly until it comes to the boil. Meanwhile put the eggs and egg yolk (if used) into a mixing bowl with the sugar (the extra yolk makes the custard more creamy but is not essential) and beat them together with the vanilla essence. Stir the hot milk slowly on to the egg mixture, whisking all the time, then strain this into the dish containing the apricot jam.

Cover with a piece of greaseproof paper, taking care it does not touch the custard, and bake the pudding in a slow oven, at *Gas Mark 2 or 300 degrees F or 150 degrees C,* for 1 hour to 1 hour 15 minutes, until the custard is just set.

To decorate the pudding
When the baked custard is cold whip the cream and milk until it is light and fluffy. Spread over the surface and top with a little grated chocolate.

Kissel

This is a delicious thickened mixture of fruits, very good with junket or natural yoghurt.

For 6 to 8 people
4 oz/125 g redcurrants
4 oz/125 g blackcurrants
12 oz/375 g cherries
1 pint/600 ml water
8 oz/250 g granulated sugar
1 lb/500 g raspberries
Arrowroot
A sprinkling of granulated sugar

Remove the stalks from the redcurrants and blackcurrants. Remove stalks and stones from the cherries. Put the water and sugar into a fairly large pan and dissolve the sugar over a low heat. Bring this syrup to the boil and add the currants and cherries and simmer them very gently for about 10 minutes. Add the raspberries, bring to the boil then turn off the heat. Drain the juice and measure it.

To each ½ pint/300 ml of juice allow 1 level tablespoon of arrowroot. Blend the arrowroot with enough cold water to make a smooth cream, stir this into the juice and then put it back in the pan and stir it over a gentle heat until it comes to the boil, it will clear as it thickens. Pour the thickened juice over the fruit, sprinkle it with a little granulated sugar to prevent a skin forming and cover the bowl. Turn into a glass bowl when cold.

Note: Although this is a pudding, it is excellent for breakfast with a cereal or muesli so that the short season of fresh fruit can be enjoyed at most meals.

To use as a pie filling This recipe makes a very good pie filling, allow double quantity of arrowroot to make the juice thicker. It can be frozen in containers to fill pies for winter use.

Apple Maraschino

(Illustrated on page 76)

For 6 or 7 people
4 oz / 125 g granulated sugar
*1 (12-oz / 339-g) can pineapple
  cubes*
Water
*2 lb / 1 kg small eating apples
  (Coxes are ideal)*
12 maraschino cherries
½ oz / 15 g angelica
2 firm bananas
*2 teaspoons maraschino liqueur,
  (optional)*

Put the sugar into a small, deep pan with the juice from the pineapple cubes and enough water to make up ½ pint/300 ml of liquid. Put the pan over a low heat until the sugar has dissolved. Meanwhile, peel the apples with a potato peeler and remove the cores, leaving the apples whole. As soon as the sugar has dissolved, bring the syrup to the boil and then poach the apples in it, a few at a time; they will take between 5 and 10 minutes each depending on their ripeness and size. Turn them over once during cooking, then remove and put them on one side to cool while poaching the remaining apples.

When all the apples are cooked, allow the remaining syrup to boil fast for 4 to 5 minutes to reduce it, then remove it from the heat. Cut the cherries in half and dice the angelica (this is easier to do if washed under warm water first which will soften it); add to the syrup with the peeled and diced bananas and the pineapple cubes. Stir in the maraschino liqueur (if used) and pour over the cooled apples. Chill well for several hours before serving.

To freeze Apples cooked in a syrup in this way freeze well; for use, allow to thaw overnight in the refrigerator. Add the banana after thawing.

Fresh Pear Delight

For 4 people
3 ripe dessert pears
2 egg whites
2 level teaspoons caster sugar
¼ pint / 150 ml double cream
1 gingernut biscuit, crumbled

Peel, core and dice the pears. Whip the egg whites until they are very stiff then whisk in the caster sugar until stiff again. Whip the cream until it will hold its shape, then fold in the egg whites. Add the pears to the mixture, then pile into a dish and sprinkle the top with the crumbled gingernut biscuit.

Gooseberries and Junket

Gooseberries are sweeter for cooking while they are still hard and bright green, so if you grow your own don't leave them on the bush too long. The elder flowers give a wonderful fragrant flavour.

For 4 or 5 people
8 oz/250 g gooseberries
½ pint/300 ml water
6 oz/175 g to 8 oz/250 g
 granulated sugar
2 heads of elder flowers (optional)
FOR THE JUNKET
1 pint/600 ml milk
2 teaspoons essence of rennet
 (less makes a softer set)
2 teaspoons caster sugar
Nutmeg

Top and tail the gooseberries with a small pair of scissors, then put them in a colander and rinse them well under cold water; this removes any dirt and tops and tails that have fallen amongst them.

Put the water and sugar into a fairly large pan, stir over a gentle heat until the sugar has dissolved then bring this syrup to a quick boil. Boil for 1 minute, then add the gooseberries. Allow the syrup to boil up quickly round the gooseberries then turn the heat to very low and allow the gooseberries to poach very gently until they are tender; some varieties are cooked when they have been brought to the boil.

Wash the elder flowers (if used), then plunge them head-first into the poaching liquid, leave them for 2 minutes then lift them out again. When they have cooled slightly turn the gooseberries into a bowl.

Note: Use this method for all stewed fruit when you want to keep it whole.

To make the junket Put the milk into a pan and warm it over a low heat. Mix the rennet and sugar in the dish in which the junket is to be set and by that time the milk will be warm enough – it should only be blood heat. Stir the milk on to the rennet and sugar, then grate a little nutmeg on to the surface and leave the junket to set. It will be set by the time the milk is cold; it is best not put in a refrigerator.

Note: Make sure the rennet essence is fresh; if it is stale the junket will not 'junk'.

Fresh Apricot Soufflé (see page 96)

92

Party Bananas

For 6 people
6 bananas
¼ pint / 150 ml double cream
A little top of the milk
Sugar to sweeten
A drop of vanilla essence
A few chocolate nibs

Lay each banana on its side and remove a strip of skin about ¾ inch / 1.5 cm wide from the full length of the fruit, except for about ½ inch / 1 cm at each end.

Whip the double cream and add just enough top of the milk to keep the cream light and fluffy. Sweeten it lightly and flavour very sparingly with vanilla essence. Fill a piping bag, fitted with a star pipe, with the cream and pipe a squiggle of cream down the skinned section of each banana. Just before serving, sprinkle the cream with a few chocolate nibs.

These bananas are best eaten with teaspoons.

Jubilee Turkey, Sherry Trifle (see pages 107, 110)

Strawberry Racer

(Illustrated on page 111)
The outsize wine glass shown in the photograph holds 1¼ pints / 750 ml of liquid.

For 3 or 4 people
8 oz / 250 g ripe strawberries
1 level tablespoon icing sugar, sifted
1 teaspoon brandy
2 oz / 50 g brown breadcrumbs
2 oz / 50 g demerara sugar
¼ pint / 150 ml double cream
¼ pint / 150 ml natural yoghurt
3 or 4 wine glasses to serve

Reserve 3 or 4 strawberries, then hull and halve the rest and divide them between the serving glasses. Sprinkle the icing sugar over the strawberries and sprinkle the brandy over the top to flavour the strawberries.

Mix the brown breadcrumbs and demerara sugar together and sprinkle them over the strawberries. Beat the double cream lightly until it will just hold its shape. Fold in the yoghurt. Pour the mixture on top of the crumbs and decorate each with a whole strawberry.

Note: When strawberries are at their peak make some:

Chocolate Strawberry Cups
(Illustrated on page 111)
Use 7 oz / 200 g of melted chocolate to coat the inside of 10 double-thickness paper cups. Leave to set, then carefully peel away paper. Mix 4 oz / 125 g of cake crumbs with the juice of ½ a lemon and 3 tablespoons of strawberry jam. Divide this mixture between the chocolate cups. Top with a strawberry and a swirl of double cream.

Fresh Apricot Soufflé

There is really no need to have a soufflé dish – a glass bowl, filled to the brim, with a border of piped cream, achieves a very pretty effect. (See page 102 for preparing soufflé dish.)

(Illustrated on page 93)

For 5 or 6 people
FOR THE APRICOT PURÉE
8 oz/250 g fresh apricots
1 level tablespoon granulated sugar
2 tablespoons water
FOR THE SOUFFLÉ MIXTURE
The juice of a large lemon
½ oz/15 g gelatine
3 eggs
3 oz/75 g caster sugar
¼ pint/150 ml double cream
A 2-pint/1.15-litre glass dish
FOR THE DECORATION
¼ pint/150 ml double cream
2 tablespoons milk
½ oz/15 g flaked almonds, lightly toasted

Halve the apricots and remove the stones. Put the fruit into a pan with the sugar and water and stew gently until it is tender. Purée the fruit in either a blender or through a Mouli vegetable mill or sieve; the yield should be about ½ pint/300 ml.

Put the lemon juice into a small pan, sprinkle the gelatine evenly over the surface and leave the pan on one side for the gelatine to soften.

Separate the eggs, putting the yolks into one fairly large bowl and the whites into another. Add the caster sugar and the warm apricot purée to the yolks and whisk until the mixture becomes thick, creamy and much lighter in colour. This takes less time with an electric mixer than it does by hand. You will find that a warm purée speeds this process.

Dissolve the gelatine over a low heat and stir it into the mixture while it is still warm. Whip the cream lightly until it will almost hold its shape and fold it into the mixture.

When the mixture is cold and just starting to set whisk the egg whites until they are light and fluffy, but not dry and stiff. Stir a tablespoon into the mixture, then lightly fold in the rest. This softens the mixture, making the ingredients combine more easily. Pour the mixture into the dish and leave it to set.

To decorate the soufflé Whip the cream and milk lightly until it will just hold its shape then, using a palette knife, spread about a quarter over the top of the soufflé, leaving a wavy effect. Put the remaining cream into a piping bag with a star pipe attached. Pipe rosettes round the edge of the soufflé. Sprinkle a few flaked almonds on top of each rosette of cream.

The soufflé may be left overnight, but is best eaten within 1 or 2 hours while the texture is soft and fluffy.

To freeze The soufflé freezes beautifully with the cream decoration, but add the almonds just before serving as they will soften in the freezer. Thaw at room temperature for 3 to 4 hours or 12 hours in the refrigerator.

Using other kinds of fruit
Many fruits, fresh, canned or

frozen and thawed, may be used for the soufflé as long as you use $\frac{1}{2}$ pint/300 ml of fairly thick purée. Plums, gooseberries, red-currants, blackcurrants, black-berries, damsons and cranberries should be cooked to a purée like the apricots, but strawberries and raspberries need not be cooked, merely sieved.

Chilled Rhubarb Cheesecake

A very economical cheesecake, especially if you grow your own rhubarb.

Cuts into 8 slices
FOR THE BASE
3 oz/75 g butter
4 oz/125 g digestive biscuits, crushed
FOR THE FILLING
1 lb/500 g rhubarb
$\frac{1}{2}$ oz/15 g gelatine
8 oz/250 g cottage cheese
$\frac{1}{4}$ pint/150 ml soured cream
6 oz/175 g caster sugar
2 eggs
An 8-inch/20-cm spring-clip tin or a 9-inch/23-cm flan tin

Melt the butter, stir in the biscuit crumbs, mix together and turn the mixture into the tin. Press it evenly into the base; a flat potato-masher or the back of a large spoon is ideal for this. Wipe the rhubarb, cut it into pieces and put it into a pan with 1 tablespoon of water; cover and cook it gently to a soft pulp. Sieve the pulp then cool the resulting purée. Put two tablespoons of water into a small pan, sprinkle the gelatine over the water and leave on one side for the gelatine to soften.

Sieve the cottage cheese and beat in the soured cream. Stir in the rhubarb purée and the sugar. Separate the eggs and beat the yolks into the mixture. Completely dissolve the gelatine over a very low heat and stir it into the mixture. Whip the egg whites till they are stiff but still have a moist and shiny ap-pearance. Beat one tablespoon into the mixture then fold the rest in very lightly. Turn the mixture into the tin and leave to set. When set, loosen carefully round the edge with a knife then remove the outside of the tin and serve the cheesecake on the base. *Note :* Other fruits may be chosen; use $\frac{1}{2}$ pint/300 ml purée as for the rhubarb purée.

To freeze Freeze the cheesecake in the tin. Allow 2 hours at room temperature for it to thaw.

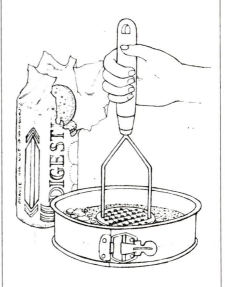

Rum Cream with Cherry Sauce Topping

For 6 to 8 people

3 eggs
4 oz / 125 g caster sugar
2 level teaspoons gelatine
4 tablespoons cold water
½ pint / 300 ml double cream
3 or 4 teaspoons rum
FOR THE CHERRY SAUCE
TOPPING
*1 (14-oz / 410-g) can black
   cherries*
2 level teaspoons arrowroot

Separate the eggs. Put the yolks and the caster sugar into a mixing bowl and beat together until very light in colour. Sprinkle the gelatine over the water in a small pan and leave for 1 to 2 minutes to soften. Dissolve gelatine over a very gentle heat without allowing it to boil, then whisk it into the egg yolk and sugar mixture. Stir in the cream and the rum. Beat the egg whites stiffly and stir 2 teaspoons into the mixture. Fold in the remaining egg white very lightly. Turn the mixture into a dish, and leave it in a cool place.

To make the cherry topping
Drain the cherry juice into a measuring jug to make just under ½ pint / 300 ml. Blend the arrowroot in a little of the juice, then add it to the remainder. Put it into a pan and stir until the juice comes to the boil; as it does this it will clear. Stone the cherries with the tip of a potato peeler and add them to the juice. Cool before pouring over the rum cream.

Blackcurrant Mousse

For 6 or 7 people

*8 oz / 250 g blackcurrants, fresh or
   frozen*
¼ pint / 150 ml water
1 blackcurrant jelly square
4 eggs
6 oz / 175 g caster sugar
FOR THE DECORATION
¼ pint / 150 ml double cream
¼ pint / 150 ml single cream
A few blackcurrants to decorate

String and wash the blackcurrants then put them into a pan with the water and cook them gently to a soft pulp. Cut up the jelly square and stir it into the currants until it is melted. Sieve the mixture and leave this purée to cool. Meanwhile separate the yolks of the eggs from the whites and beat the yolks with the sugar until they are light and fluffy. Stir in the cooled blackcurrant purée. Whisk the egg whites stiffly and lightly fold them into the mixture. Turn the mousse into a glass bowl in a cool place to set.

Whisk the creams together until they are light and fluffy and spread half over the surface of the pudding. Fill a piping bag, fitted with a star pipe, with the remaining cream and pipe crisscross lines over the top. Decorate with a few blackcurrants.
Note: This mousse freezes very well; if eaten soon after it comes out of the freezer it becomes a delicious blackcurrant ice cream.

If you prefer, use ½ oz / 15 g powdered gelatine dissolved in the blackcurrant juice instead of the jelly and add an extra 2 oz / 50 g caster sugar.

Banana Cream Jelly

For 4 people
1 lemon or lime jelly
4 bananas
1 (5-fl oz/142-ml) carton double cream
A few drops of cooking oil
A straight-sided soufflé dish, about 6 inches/15 cm in diameter, of 1½-pint/900-ml capacity

Cut up the jelly square into a measuring jug and cover with boiling water as directed on the packet. Stir until dissolved, then leave the jelly until it is almost cold.

Brush a few drops of cooking oil round the inside of the soufflé dish. Line the base with a circle of greaseproof paper, cut to fit exactly.

Pour a little of the jelly into the dish and put it in the refrigerator to set quickly. Peel and slice one banana and arrange 7 slices round the base of the dish on top of the set jelly. Run just a little jelly over the banana slices and leave to set.

Peel the remaining bananas and mash them with a fork. Whip the double cream lightly then fold it into the bananas, and add the rest of the jelly. Pour this gently on to the banana slices and leave it to set.

To turn out the jelly, loosen round the top with a knife then dip the base of the dish into hot water for a few seconds just to ease the base. Put a few drops of cold water on to a plate, invert the jelly, then slip the jelly into the centre of the plate; you will find it moves quite easily on the moist plate. Peel the greaseproof paper from the top.

Use the day it is made, as the banana tends to discolour.

Syllabub

This is a lightly whipped wine-flavoured cream; here we chose an elderberry wine for it, although any white or rosé wine or cider makes delicious syllabub. Serve with fresh or poached fruit, Mincemeat Jalousie or Kissel (see pages 89 and 90).

For 8 to 10 people
¼ pint/150 ml elderberry wine
3 oz/75 g caster sugar
The juice of 1 lemon
½ pint/300 ml double cream

Put the wine, caster sugar and lemon juice into a mixing bowl.

Add the double cream to the wine mixture gradually while beating with an electric or rotary beater to a light and fluffy texture. Turn into an attractive bowl, leaving the surface in light folds.

Note: This is often served in wine glasses, with sponge finger biscuits.

Yoghurt Pudding

A most refreshing pudding and, surrounded with fresh raspberry leaves, an ideal choice for a party.

For 5 people

1 (8-oz/250-g) can raspberries
½ oz/15 g gelatine
2 oz/50 g caster sugar
1 pint/600 ml natural yoghurt
Juice of 1 lemon
A few drops of pink colouring
¼ pint/150 ml double cream
A few fresh raspberries for decoration
A 1½-pint/900-ml jelly mould

Drain the raspberries and reserve the juice. Sprinkle the gelatine over the fruit juice. Dissolve in a small pan over a gentle heat without allowing it to boil, then add the sugar. Blend the natural yoghurt and the lemon juice together and gradually stir in the gelatine mixture, adding a few drops of pink colouring. Allow the mixture to cool, and just before it sets stir in the raspberries.

Rub the inside of the jelly mould with a little cooking oil and pour in the mixture. Leave to set.

Turn out the yoghurt pudding on to a serving dish, lightly whip the cream and pour just over half of it on top of the pudding; it will slightly coat the sides. Serve the remaining cream separately.

Cream Meringues

Makes about 12 filled meringues

A few drops of cooking oil
Flour
3 egg whites
6 oz/175 g caster sugar
FOR THE FILLING
½ pint/300 ml double cream
2 tablespoons milk
12 paper cases

First prepare the trays on which the meringues are to be baked; rub a few drops of cooking oil over the upturned surface, then dust with flour. Tip each tray and knock it sharply on the edge so that only a light dusting of flour is left on the surface.

Put the egg whites into a large, clean, grease-free bowl and beat them, slowly at first, then faster as they begin to thicken. A large wire whisk is best for this, though a rotary beater can be used and, of course, if you have an electric mixer it is ideal. Keep lifting the whisk out of the mixture, and when the egg white which clings to it stands in a straight peak with no bend, then some sugar can be added.

Add 3 level tablespoons of the measured sugar and beat this thoroughly into the egg whites until the original stiff consistency is reached. Lightly fold in the remaining sugar with a metal spoon.

Fill a piping bag, fitted with a large star pipe, with the meringue mixture. Hold the bag in your right hand and, keeping the mixture below the pressure of the hand, pipe out meringues on to the tray. Put the meringues into a very slow oven, set at the lowest *Gas Mark or about 180 degrees F or 100 degrees C.*

Bake the meringues for about 4 hours. If they start to become tinged with colour, open the oven door very slightly. After this time the meringues should have become firm, dry and crisp to the centre. Take them out of the oven and lift them off the trays.

To fill the meringues Put the meringues in pairs in paper cases; this is the easiest way to fill them. Whip the cream with the milk until it just holds its shape then put it into the piping bag fitted with star pipe and pipe the cream between the meringues.

Note: Although cream-filled meringues should be eaten within a few hours of filling, the meringue shells (unfilled) keep very well in an airtight tin, and are useful for instant entertaining.

If you have no piping bag place tablespoons of meringue on to the baking trays.

Brandied Raspberries

For 3 people

1 (14½-oz/410-g) can raspberries
3 level teaspoons arrowroot
2 teaspoons brandy
1 (4-fl oz/125-g) carton double cream
Grated nutmeg
Serve with assorted biscuits

Drain the raspberries. Blend the arrowroot with a little of the raspberry juice in a pan, then add the rest of the juice and stir until it comes to the boil and thickens. Add the brandy and the raspberries and leave until cold.

Divide between 3 individual glasses. Whip the cream and, using a piping bag fitted with a star pipe, pipe a good whirl of cream on to each. Dust the tops with grated nutmeg. Serve the assorted biscuits separately.

Variation

Cherry Napoleon Use a can of black cherries instead of raspberries.

Orange Soufflé

For 5 people

4 eggs
4 oz / 25 g caster sugar
1 (6¼-fl oz / 175-ml) can frozen
  concentrated orange juice,
  thawed
¼ pint / 150 ml double cream
½ oz / 15 g gelatine
3 tablespoons water
A 2-pint / 1.15-litre soufflé dish
Greaseproof paper and string
FOR THE DECORATION
¼ pint / 150 ml double cream
2 level tablespoons chopped
  browned almonds

First prepare the soufflé dish. Cut a doubled strip of grease-proof paper so that it is long enough to circle it and comes about 3 inches / 7.5 cm above the top of the dish. Tie the strip firmly around the outside of the dish with string.

Separate the eggs; put the yolks into a bowl with the sugar and whisk with an electric whisk until thick and creamy. Whisk in the orange juice, undiluted. Whisk the cream until it will just hold its shape when allowed to drop from the end of the beater, then fold this into the orange mixture.

Put the water in a small pan and carefully sprinkle the gelatine over it; leave it to soak for a few minutes then place it over a gentle heat and allow it to dissolve, without boiling; stir it into the mixture.

Whisk the egg whites until fairly thick and snowy; take out one tablespoon and stir this into the mixture, then very carefully fold in the rest of the whites. Pour the mixture into the prepared soufflé dish and leave to set, either in a cool place overnight or in the fridge for a few hours. (We cover the surface loosely with a polythene bag to prevent a skin forming.)

When the soufflé is set, carefully remove the paper collar. Whip the cream lightly and spread a little around the side of the soufflé. Fill the piping bag, fitted with a large star pipe, with the rest of the cream. Form the almonds into a ring on a piece of greaseproof paper, place the dish in the centre and with a palette knife press the nuts on to the cream-covered side of the soufflé.

Pipe 6 large rosettes of cream around the outside edge of the soufflé top.

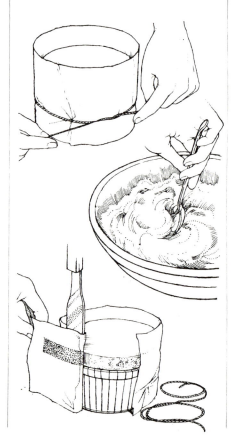

Party Fare

Planned spontaneity is the secret behind successful informal entertaining. Plans must be laid, to ensure good and sufficient food and drink for the guests invited.

Our suggestions are mainly for savoury dishes of the finger and fork variety, not always easy to estimate for, bearing economy in mind.

A variety of puddings always looks interesting and festive and there are four in this chapter for larger numbers, Trifle, Melon Fruit Salad, Lime and Lemon Cheesecake and Mince Pies. Serve a selection of these according to the numbers.

Ploughman's Party

Good for a fund-raising affair or an easy buffet to organise for large numbers, for instance for a cricket club dance.

For a large party provide:
Bread and cheese Buy a large quantity of both and allow 3 oz/75 g cheese and 2 rolls or 2 thick slices of bread per person. A selection of crusty and whole-wheat loaves is attractive. For large numbers choose large wedges or miniature-type whole cheeses. A whole Edam surrounded by wedges of farmhouse cheeses makes a handsome display.

Pickled onions
Chutney
Celery
Watercress
Plenty of softened butter
An apple for everyone – green, yellow, russet and red-skinned – in an attractive big basket
Cider
Tea or Coffee

Tea

For 1 gallon/4.5 litres of tea to drink allow 2 oz/50 g to 3 oz/75 g of tea or 20 tea bags (depending on the strength required); allow 1½ pints/900 ml to 2 pints/1.15 litres of milk and 1 lb/500 g of sugar.

Coffee

For coffee allow 8 oz/250 g fresh-ground coffee (or 16 level table-spoons of instant coffee) to 1 gallon/4.5 litres of boiling water, and 3 pints/1.75 litres of milk and 1 lb/500g of sugar.

1 gallon/4.5 litres of tea or coffee is enough for 20 people.

Allow 1 bottle of cider for every 5 or 6 guests.

Guests could be asked to bring enough mince pies (see page 113) for themselves. Get them to leave all the pies near the cheese so that everyone can help them-selves, either to their own – or to nicer ones if they're lucky!

Home-Made Mustard

(Blender method)

2 oz/50 g white mustard seeds
2 oz/50 g black mustard seeds
¼ pint/150 ml white wine vinegar
3 level tablespoons clear honey
1 level teaspoon salt
¼ level teaspoon ground cinnamon
A little extra vinegar, if necessary

Put the mustard seeds and vinegar into a bowl, cover and leave for about 36 hours to soften.

Transfer the seeds and vinegar to a blender goblet. Add the honey, salt and cinnamon and blend them at high speed until the mixture is thick. Add a little more vinegar if the mixture seems too thick. Put the mustard into the small jars and cover them with the plastic tops.

Party Pizzas

Pizzas can be served hot or cold and either way they are good served with a simple green salad. They are also economical. For a party, have a selection of different salads and perhaps red Chianti to drink.

The pizza mixture is similar to a scone dough and the less handling it has the better. Pizzas freeze beautifully.

All the recipes below can be cut into 6 generous slices.

FOR THE BASIC TOMATO
MIXTURE
2 medium-sized onions
2 teaspoons cooking oil
1 (14-oz/396-g) can tomatoes
Salt and freshly ground black pepper
1 level teaspoon dried oregano
(basil or marjoram could be used
instead; if using fresh herbs
allow 1 heaped teaspoon, finely
chopped)
QUICK PIZZA BASE
6 oz/175 g self-raising flour
½ level teaspoon salt
1 oz/25 g margarine
6 tablespoons milk
1 small egg, beaten
Cooking oil for brushing the tin
A 9-inch/23-cm loose-based flan tin

Peel and slice the onions finely. Heat the oil in a large frying pan, add the onions and cook gently for a few minutes until they are soft. Add the contents of the can of tomatoes and cook until the mixture is reduced to a thick pulp. Season the mixture with salt, freshly ground black pepper and the oregano. Allow to cool.

While the tomato mixture is cooling make the quick scone base. Sift the flour with the salt into a mixing bowl. Cut the margarine into small pieces and rub these into the flour with the tips of your fingers. Make a well in the centre of the flour and fat mixture and pour in the milk and beaten egg. Gradually stir in the mixture from round the edge of the bowl until a dough is formed. Do not knead the mixture, but turn it straight into the prepared flan tin and pat it gently over the base; top with the prepared tomato mixture and one of the toppings (see following recipes).

Bake at *Gas Mark 6 or 400 degrees F or 200 degrees C,* for 30 minutes.

Before serving, remove the side of the flan tin. To do this, stand the pizza in the tin on a bowl or can that is smaller than the base, then lower the flan ring so that it drops down round the can and lift the pizza on the tin base on to the serving board.

To freeze Wrap the pizzas in foil before freezing. To reheat straight from the freezer, open up the top, and allow about 30 minutes at *Gas Mark 5 or 375 degrees F or 190 degrees C.*

Cheese Pizza

Quick Pizza Base and tomato mixture (see page 104)
8 oz / 250 g cheese (the traditional cheese is Mozzarella)
1 (2-oz / 50-g) can anchovy fillets
5 black olives
Oil

Cut the cheese in thin slices with a very sharp knife and arrange these neatly over the top of the

tomato mixture, overlapping them slightly in the centre.

Drain the oil from the anchovies, cut each anchovy into half down its length, and arrange them carefully in circles, decreasing in size from the outer edge towards the centre. Use remaining anchovies to divide pizza into 4 or 6 sections. Halve the olives, remove the stones, and arrange them round the edge of the pizza. Brush the top with oil. Bake as described for basic recipe.

Tuna Pizza

Quick Pizza Base and tomato mixture (see page 104)
1 (7-oz / 200-g) can tuna in oil
A few black olives
Cooking oil

Turn the tuna fish into a bowl and flake it with a fork; scatter the flakes over the top of the tomato mixture. Halve and stone the olives and arrange them on top. Brush liberally with oil then bake as described for basic recipe.

Mushroom Pizza

Quick Pizza Base and tomato mixture (see page 104)
8 oz / 250 g button mushrooms, washed and sliced
Cooking oil

Scatter the sliced mushrooms over the top of the tomato mixture and brush liberally with oil. Bake as described for basic recipe.

Cockle Pizza

Quick Pizza Base and tomato
mixture (see page 104)
7 oz / 200 g frozen cockles, thawed
Cooking oil

Scatter the cockles over the top
of the tomato mixture and brush
liberally with oil. Bake as described for basic recipe.

Ham and Cheese Fingers

Makes about 28
6 oz / 175 g cooked ham, minced or
    finely chopped
8 oz / 250 g Cheddar cheese, grated
1 onion, peeled and very finely
    chopped
Salt and freshly ground pepper
1 large packet of frozen puff pastry,
    thawed
A little beaten egg for the glaze

Mix the ham, grated cheese and
chopped onion. Season the mixture carefully with salt and
freshly ground black pepper.

Roll the pastry into a rectangle 14 inches/35 cm long by
12 inches/30 cm wide and cut it
down the centre to divide into
2 equal lengths. Spread one
piece with the filling and put the
other piece on top; press it down
firmly. Brush the top with beaten
egg and cut in fingers about
1 inch/2.5 cm wide by 3 inches/
8 cm long. Transfer them to
baking trays and leave them in
a cool place for a few minutes
before baking.

Bake the fingers in a hot oven,
*Gas Mark 6 or 400 degrees F or 200
degrees C*, for 20 minutes.

Apple Sausage Rolls

**Makes 36 cocktail-sized
sausage rolls**
FOR QUICK FLAKY PASTRY
10 oz / 300 g plain flour
A good pinch of salt
8 oz / 250 g margarine, in a hard
    block from the refrigerator
FOR THE FILLING
1 lb / 500 g sausagemeat
¼ pint / 150 ml apple purée, slightly
    sweetened
FOR THE GLAZE
A little beaten egg

Sift the flour and salt into a
mixing bowl. Grate the margarine into the flour then mix it
in with a knife. Add just enough
cold water to make a dough a
little softer than that for shortcrust pastry. Wrap the pastry
and leave it in a cool place for
30 minutes.

Divide the sausagemeat into
three and roll each piece into a
12-inch/30-cm sausage, using a
little flour to prevent sticking.

Roll out the pastry and trim it
carefully to a 12-inch/30-cm by
15-inch/38-cm rectangle; cut the
rectangle into 3, 5-inch/13-cm
by 12-inch/30-cm strips. Spread
the centre of each strip with the
apple purée, then lay a piece of
sausagemeat on top. Moisten
the edge of each piece of pastry
with water and roll it up with the
sausage inside. Brush the surface
of the pastry with beaten egg to
make the glaze. Cut each long
strip into 12, 1-inch/2.5-cm
sausage-type rolls and leave
them to rest for 30 minutes. Bake
in a hot oven, *Gas Mark 7 or 425
degrees F or 220 degrees C*, for
15 minutes.

Note: These can of course be made larger, when they will take a little longer to bake; they freeze beautifully.

Jubilee Turkey

(Illustrated on page 94)

Cooked ahead and easy to serve, it is ideal for entertaining up to 20 people.

For 20
1 14-lb/6.25-kg to 16-lb/7.25-kg turkey
2 bay leaves, 2 good sprigs of thyme and a good sprig of tarragon if available, or 2 bouquet garni
FOR THE SAUCE
8 oz/250 g streaky bacon
3 medium-sized onions
1 lb/500 g button mushrooms
10 oz/300 g butter
8 oz/250 g plain flour
1 (2-lb/3-oz/1.75-kg) can tomatoes
3½ pints/2 litres turkey stock
Salt and pepper
Juice of ½ lemon
A little Worcester sauce to taste
2 oz/50 g chopped parsley

Wipe the turkey and wash the giblets. Put the herbs or bouquet garni inside the bird and roast it breast downwards for 4 hours at *Gas Mark 4 or 350 degrees F or 190 degrees C*, until done.
Allow the bird to cool. Cut off the flesh, removing the bones, skin and giblets, and cut the meat into fork-sized pieces. Make the stock with the turkey bones, skin and giblets. Put these in a large pan and cover them with water, add salt and pepper and simmer gently for

about 1½ hours. Strain into a bowl.

To make the sauce Cut the rinds from the bacon and snip the rashers into small pieces. Fry these without extra fat in a fairly large pan, until they are crisp. Peel and slice the onions, wash, drain and dry the mushrooms. Add 2 oz/50 g butter to the bacon and melt it. Add the chopped onions and cook them very gently until they are just tender, then add the mushrooms and cook them for a few minutes with the onions and bacon. Remove them from the heat.
Melt the remaining butter in a very large pan. Remove from the heat and stir in the flour, which should make a soft smooth paste. Then stir in the stock and cook over a very gentle heat until the mixture is smooth; you can use a wire whisk to disperse any small lumps. Increase the heat and continue to stir until the sauce thickens and comes to the boil. Simmer it for a few minutes then add the contents of the can of tomatoes and season carefully with salt and pepper, lemon juice and Worcester sauce. Stir in the bacon, onion and mushroom mixture. Add the turkey and turn it carefully into the sauce.
Heat the turkey gently, being careful not to break up the pieces. Transfer the turkey to warmed serving dishes and scatter the top thickly with chopped parsley. Serve with a border of creamed potato or with minted new potatoes and braised courgettes or green beans.

Spaghetti Sauce

Makes 5 pints/3 litres, enough for 20 people

4 tablespoons cooking oil
2 lb/1 kg onions, peeled and sliced
2 cloves of garlic
2 level tablespoons paprika
2 level tablespoons plain flour
3 (1-lb 8-oz/790-oz) cans tomatoes
Salt and pepper
1 level teaspoon dried basil, marjoram or oregano

Heat the oil in a large pan then add the onions, cover and cook them for about 5 minutes. Crush the garlic and add it to the onions and continue cooking them until they start to soften, stirring frequently. Stir in the paprika and flour and cook for 1 to 2 minutes.

Stir in the contents of the cans of tomatoes and stir the sauce until it comes to the boil then season it carefully with salt and pepper and the herbs. Simmer the sauce for at least 30 minutes to thicken it and concentrate the flavour.

To freeze Freeze it in the quantities you are most likely to require. Allow to thaw overnight.

Spaghetti quantities Allow 2 oz/50 g to 3 oz/75 g spaghetti per person, depending on age and appetite. Cook as directed on the packet, and serve it in bowls; cover with plenty of sauce and sprinkle the top of each helping liberally with grated cheese. Traditionally this should be Parmesan cheese but grated Cheddar cheese is excellent. Finish with a knob of butter on top.

Stuffed Cannelloni

Ideally this should be served with Chianti or a wine of your choice from the wide range of red and white Italian wines. This main course, planned for a supper party for 6 people, can be made in advance; served with a salad it makes very little work. It is also an ideal recipe to double up for large numbers.

1 (7-oz/200-g) can luncheon meat
1 (10-oz/300-g) can asparagus tips
12 pieces of cannelloni
FOR THE SAUCE
2 oz/50 g margarine
2 oz/50 g plain flour
2 pints/1 litre milk
6 oz/175 g Cheddar cheese, grated
Salt and pepper
A little chopped parsley

Cut the luncheon meat into 12 thin slices. Open the can of asparagus and turn the contents gently on to a plate. Wrap 2 asparagus tips in a slice of luncheon meat and slip the roll into a piece of cannelloni. If this is difficult use just one asparagus tip and add what remains to the sauce. Put the rolls into a roasting tin ready to add the sauce.

For the sauce Melt the margarine in a large pan then take it off the heat and stir in the flour. Add all the milk and bring the sauce to the boil, whisking it to keep it smooth. Simmer for 1 minute then take the pan off the heat, beat in half the cheese and season the sauce carefully with salt and pepper. Pour the sauce over the cannelloni; it will be thin at this stage but the liquid will be absorbed sufficiently by the cannelloni during cooking. Sprinkle the top with the rest of the cheese.

Bake the cannelloni in a moderate oven, *Gas Mark 4 or 350 degrees F or 180 degrees C*, for about 1 hour, then sprinkle the chopped parsley over the top.

To freeze This dish freezes well. It can be reheated from frozen and will take about an hour at *Gas Mark 4 or 350 degrees F or 180 degrees C*, but 30 minutes will be enough if it is thawed before heating.

Melon Fruit Salad

This is a useful fruit base to which you can add your own selection of fruits; ours is just a suggestion.

For 10 to 12 people
3 oranges
1 lemon
8 oz/250 g to 12 oz/375 g sugar, depending on your own taste, or the sharpness of the fruit
1 pint/600 ml water
1 green-skinned melon
4 oz/125 g black grapes
1 green-skinned apple
1 red-skinned apple
1 small punnet of strawberries
2 bananas

Using a potato peeler remove the rind from one orange and the lemon, taking as little of the white pith as possible as this will make the syrup taste bitter. Put the rind into a pan with the sugar and water. Stir the mixture over a gentle heat until all the sugar has dissolved, then bring the

syrup to the boil and boil it rapidly for 3 minutes. Strain the syrup and leave it to cool, then add the juice from both the orange and the lemon.

Cut the melon in half and remove the seeds then, using a ball cutter or a teaspoon, remove the melon from its skin and put the balls straight into the syrup. Keep one half of the melon skin for decorating the dish.

Using a sharp knife, cut the skin spirally off the remaining 2 oranges, removing the white pith as well. Cut down between each section, removing the segments, and add these to the salad. Cut the grapes in half and remove the pips, cut each apple into quarters and remove the cores but do not peel them, just slice them thinly. Add the fruit together with the hulled strawberries. Leave the fruit for at least 30 minutes and just before serving add the sliced banana. Cut the melon skin into thin wedges and surround the bowl with them so that the points overlap the dish.

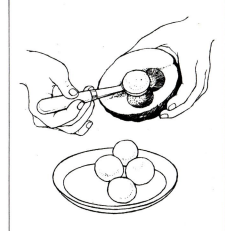

Sherry Trifle

(Illustrated on page 94)

For 10 people

8 oz / 250 g sponge, Swiss roll or a
 packet of trifle sponges
3 level tablespoons raspberry jam
2 (15-oz / 425-g) cans fruit
 cocktail or canned raspberries or
 strawberries
4 tablespoons sherry
2 pints / 1.15 litres milk for the
 custard
4 level tablespoons custard powder
4 oz / 125 g caster sugar
½ pint / 300 ml double cream
3 tablespoons milk
6 glacé cherries, halved
12 diamonds of angelica
6 almonds, blanched and toasted
A large piping bag and a large
 star pipe
A 4½-pint / 2.5-litre glass dish

Cut the sponge into small cubes, put these into the glass dish and dot with the jam. Open the cans of fruit and spread the fruit over the sponge. Mix the sherry with the juice and pour this too over the sponge.

Make the custard with the milk as directed on the packet but instead of adding the sugar, sprinkle it over the cooked custard to prevent a skin forming while it cools and cover with a lid. When it is cold beat in the sugar and pour the custard over the fruit.

When the custard is completely cold whip the cream and milk together until they just hold their shape. With the star pipe attached, fill the piping bag with cream and pipe a trellis design of cream over the custard. Pipe round the outer edge and decorate this alternately with half glacé cherries, diamonds of angelica and the halved browned almonds.

Note: The trifle can be made in advance and covered with cling film to prevent a skin forming. Decorate it with the whipped cream during the morning of the party.

For children The sherry can be left out of the trifle, or you can make it in two dishes, adding sherry to the one for the grown-ups.

Strawberry Racer, Chocolate Strawberry Cups, Strawberry Cinnamon Shortcakes (see pages 95, 125)

HONEY
FLAPJ

COLATE
& PIES

Mince Pies

Makes about 12 to 15 small pies
8 oz/250 g plain flour
A good pinch of salt
2 oz/75 g margarine
2 oz/75 g lard
Cold water to mix
1 lb/500 g mincemeat
A little lightly beaten egg white
A dusting of caster sugar
Round tartlet tins

Sift the flour with the salt, then rub the fats into the flour. Add just enough cold water to the pastry mix to make a stiff dough. Roll out the pastry to about an eighth of an inch in thickness and cut out rounds just larger than the tartlet tins. Line the tins with the pastry. Put a good teaspoon of mincemeat into each.

Cut rounds of pastry to cover the tops of the pies, and using a little water to moisten the meeting edges, press each cover and base firmly together.

Brush the top of each pie with lightly beaten egg white and sprinkle with caster sugar.

Bake the mince pies in a moderately hot oven, *Gas Mark 5 or 375 degrees F or 190 degrees C,* for about 20 minutes. Slip them out of the tins.

Lime and Lemon Cheesecake

Cuts into 10 to 12 slices
8 oz/250 g digestive biscuits
4 oz/125 g butter
1 lime jelly
½ pint/300 ml water
1 lemon
1 lb/500 g curd or cream cheese
¼ pint/150 ml double cream
1 lime, if available, for the decoration (a lemon can be used)
1 (11-inch/28-cm) loose-based flan tin

Put the digestive biscuits into a polythene bag and crush them with a rolling pin. Melt the butter in a saucepan and stir in the crushed biscuits. Turn the mixture into the flan tin and press it out evenly.

Melt the jelly in the water over a gentle heat, then take it off the heat and allow it to cool. Grate the lemon rind finely and squeeze out the juice. Sieve the cheese if it is very lumpy, then beat in the lemon rind and the cool jelly; this is best done with a hand mixer, to make a really smooth texture. Lightly whip the cream until it will just hold its shape and fold it into the mixture. Pour into the flan case and leave to set in a cool place.

Cut the lime into thin slices and cut each slice once to the centre; twist to make a curl and arrange round the top of the cheesecake.

Teatime Scones, Chocolate Crispies, Honey Flapjacks (see pages 115, 122, 123)

Cakes and Bakes

We have almost returned to the age of the Baking Day – not Friday, or Sunday in the residual oven heat from the Sunday joint, but more often a morning or afternoon set aside to bake and to freeze the results for future use.

Home-made baking is such a good fund-raiser that we have included a selection of our favourite tray bakes designed specifically for cake stalls. The great advantages of these are their quick and easy handling. The tins are conveniently shallow to take two or three in the oven at once, and they can be stacked for freezing so they are very economical of space. On the day the tray bakes thaw quickly; cut, handle and wrap while still firm from the freezer.

Eggs for baking
In our recipes we use large eggs for their greater volume. You can use small ones if you wish, but cakes made with large eggs are not only a little bigger but keep better.

Drop Scones

Makes 20
8 oz / 250 g plain flour
1 level teaspoon bicarbonate of soda
2 level teaspoons cream of tartar
2 level tablespoons caster sugar
1 egg
Just over ¼ pint / 150 ml milk
Lard

Heat the girdle slowly and evenly. Sift together the flour, bicarbonate of soda, and cream of tartar, then stir in the caster sugar. Make a hollow in the centre of the dry ingredients; break the egg and drop it into the centre with almost all of the milk. Mix the ingredients, without beating them, to a fairly thick batter using more milk if required. Be careful not to add too much milk at the beginning.

Grease the girdle with a little lard or use a piece of paper that the lard has been wrapped in. Drop 1 tablespoon of batter on to the girdle to test the heat; if it is right, bubbles should rise in the batter after a few seconds. As soon as the surface is covered with bubbles and the scone is well risen, flip it over to brown on the other side.

Cook all the scones in the same way, re-greasing the girdle each time. When they are ready, cool the scones between the folds of a tea towel.

To freeze Stack and freeze. Thaw about 2 hours before unwrapping; they will then separate easily.

Teatime Scones

(Illustrated on page 112)

Here are 5 different kinds of scones – plain, sultana, wholewheat, treacle and cheese; it is easy to change the flavour by using a different flour or by adding dried fruit or treacle.

Makes about 25
1 lb/500 g plain flour
4 level teaspoons cream of tartar
2 level teaspoons bicarbonate of soda
A pinch of salt
3 oz/100 g margarine
2 oz/50 g caster sugar
½ pint/300 ml milk
A 2-inch/5-cm cutter
A little milk and egg beaten together to glaze the scones

Have a hot oven ready at *Gas Mark 7 or 425 degrees F or 220 degrees C*, for baking the scones. Sift the flour with the cream of tartar, bicarbonate of soda and salt into a mixing bowl and rub in the margarine. Stir in the sugar. Then, mixing quickly with your hand, add enough milk to make a soft, but not sticky dough. Turn this out on to a floured surface and, using a good dusting of flour, roll the dough to just over ¾ inch/1.5 cm thick. Stamp out scones with the cutter and put them on a baking tray. Lightly knead the

scraps together and make more scones. Brush the tops lightly with a little beaten egg and milk.

Bake the scones for about 10 minutes. When they are well risen and golden brown, take them out of the oven and allow them to cool on a rack, covered with a tea towel to keep them moist.

Variations

For the sultana scones Add 3 oz/100 g sultanas to the mixture with the sugar, then continue as for teatime scones.

For the wholewheat scones Substitute wholewheat flour for the plain flour and make exactly as for Teatime scones. A little more milk may be required.

For the treacle scones Use just under ½ pint/300 ml of milk and stir 2 level tablespoons of black treacle into it before continuing as described for Teatime scones.

For the cheese scones Add 3 oz/100 g grated cheese instead of the sugar. Split and serve buttered with grated cheese on top.

Easy cream teas for a bazaar or fête
It's a good idea to fill a baker's basket with rows of the different flavours for display. We suggest they are sold ready to eat with a paper plate and a choice of two kinds of scones. Have small paper cases each filled with a tablespoon of jam and some more filled with whipped cream.

To freeze All the scones freeze beautifully.

Quick Chocolate Sandwich Cake

4 oz/125 g self-raising flour
4 level tablespoons cocoa powder
A pinch of salt
4 oz/125 g light brown soft sugar
4 oz/125 g margarine, softened
2 tablespoons milk
2 eggs, size 2
Two 6½-inch/17-cm sandwich tins,
  brushed with melted fat and the
  bases lined with greaseproof paper
  and brushed again with melted
  fat
FOR THE FILLING
3 level tablespoons apricot jam

Sift the flour, cocoa and salt into a mixing bowl, add the sugar, margarine, milk and eggs. Beat well together for 1 minute by hand or just under 1 minute if using an electric mixer. Divide the mixture between the 2 prepared tins and bake at *Gas Mark 5 or 375 degrees F or 190 degrees C,* for 20 to 25 minutes. Leave the cakes to cool, then turn them out and remove the greaseproof paper. Sandwich them together with the apricot jam and ice them with glacé icing or any of the following toppings.

Glacé Icing

About 2 tablespoons lemon or
  orange juice or water
6 oz/175 g icing sugar, sifted

Stir the liquid with the icing sugar to make a thick coating consistency. Spread it over the top of the cake.

Butter Icing

2 oz/50 g butter, softened
4 oz/125 g icing sugar, sifted
1 tablespoon milk

Beat the butter with the icing sugar and milk until light and fluffy. Spread over the top of the cake.

Chocolate Butter Icing Substitute 3 level tablespoons of cocoa blended with 3 tablespoons of boiling water for the milk and beat into the butter with the sugar,

Coffee Butter Icing Substitute 2 level teaspoons of instant coffee powder blended with 1 tablespoon of boiling water for the milk and blend into the butter with the icing sugar.

Orange or Lemon Butter Icing Add the grated rind of 1 orange or lemon to the butter and substitute 1 tablespoon of juice for the milk.

Fudge Icing

1½ oz/50 g butter
3 oz/100 g brown soft sugar
3 tablespoons milk
3 oz/100 g icing sugar, sifted
1 teaspoon vanilla essence

Put the butter into a pan and brown it gently over the heat, then stir in the brown soft sugar and the milk. Stir over a gentle heat to dissolve the sugar, then bring it to the boil. Boil for 1 minute, cool and beat in the sifted icing sugar with the vanilla essence. Spread the icing over the cake at once as it thickens when it cools.

Note: The glacé or butter icings are sufficient to coat the top of the Quick Chocolate Sandwich Cake.

To freeze Freeze, iced or un-iced, wrapped individually. Thaw for about 2 hours.

Coconut and Cherry Loaf

When baking in a loaf-shaped tin, the measurements refer to the top of the tin.

8 oz/250 g plain flour
¼ level teaspoon salt
1½ level teaspoons baking powder
3 oz/100 g margarine
2 oz/50 g glacé cherries
3 oz/100 g granulated sugar
2 oz/50 g desiccated coconut
1 egg
¼ pint/150 ml milk
A little cooking oil
Greaseproof paper
FOR THE TOPPING
2 tablespoons sweetened condensed milk
2 tablespoons desiccated coconut
3 glacé cherries

Line the base of a 7¼-inch/17-cm by 4¾-inch/12-cm by 3-inch/7.5-cm deep loaf tin with greaseproof paper and brush it well with melted fat. Sift the flour, salt and baking powder into a large mixing bowl. Rub the margarine into the flour with the tips of your fingers until the mixture has a fine, even texture. Cut the cherries into quarters and add them with the sugar and coconut. Beat the eggs and stir gently but thoroughly into the mixture with the milk.

Turn the mixture into the prepared tin, smooth over the surface and hollow out the centre slightly.

Bake the loaf in the centre of the preheated oven *Gas Mark 3 or 325 degrees F or 160 degrees C,* for 1 hour. Ten minutes before the end of the cooking time prepare the topping. Mix the sweetened condensed milk and coconut. Halve the cherries and put them on top of the cake, then spoon the topping over and finish the baking.

The loaf is ready when a warmed thin skewer, inserted into the centre, comes out clean.

To store the loaf Wrap in foil, or put in a tin or polythene bag. The loaf keeps well. It can be sliced thinly and spread with butter.

To freeze The loaf may be sliced before freezing; this can be useful as one slice or separate slices will thaw quickly. Allow 3 hours at room temperature to thaw as the texture is rather dense.

Walnut and Chocolate Gâteau

(Illustrated on page 1)

This gâteau is a splendid centrepiece for a buffet table.

Makes 12 pieces

FOR THE BASE

4 oz/125 g butter
8 digestive biscuits, crushed to make 4 oz/125 g
4 oz/125 g chopped walnuts (broken walnuts, which are usually cheaper, can be used if you can get them)

FOR THE CAKE

4 oz/125 g margarine, softened
8 oz/250 g caster sugar
4 oz/125 g plain chocolate
2 eggs, size 2
7 oz/200 g self-raising flour
½ level teaspoon ground cinnamon
¼ level teaspoon salt
¼ pint/150 ml soured cream
¼ pint/150 ml strong black coffee (this can be made with instant coffee; use 2 level teaspoons)
A loose-based spring-clip tin 8 inches/20 cm in diameter, greased (see note at end of recipe)

FOR THE TOP AND SIDES OF THE CAKE

¼ pint/150 ml double cream
¼ pint/150 ml single cream
3 oz/100 g chopped walnuts
8 glacé cherries, roughly chopped
1 oz/25 g angelica, cut into diamonds

To make the base Melt the butter in a pan and stir in the crushed digestive biscuits and chopped walnuts, then turn them into the spring-clip tin and press them firmly to the base with a potato masher or a tablespoon.

To make the chocolate cake mixture Put the margarine into a warm mixing bowl, beat it for a few moments then beat in the caster sugar. Break the chocolate into squares, put it on a plate and melt it above a pan of hot but not boiling water or in a warm place, then beat it into the creamed mixture. Beat in the eggs, one at a time. Sift the flour, cinnamon and salt together and fold these lightly into the mixture with the soured cream and cold coffee. This makes a very soft mixture but results in a moist cake. Pour it on to the prepared biscuit base.

Bake the cake in the centre of moderate oven, *Gas Mark 4 or 350 degrees F or 180 degrees C*, for 1¼ hours. Leave the cake in the tin until it is cold. Loosen round the edge with a sharp knife and slip off the ring leaving the cake on the tin base.

To decorate the cake Whisk both the single and double creams together until they are light and fluffy and will just hold the marks of the whisk. Spread the cream over the top and side of the cake, spreading it especially thickly over the top in a swirly pattern.

Lift the cake on to a large piece of greaseproof paper, surround it with a circle of chopped walnuts and, using a palette knife, lift the nuts carefully on to the cream-covered side of the cake to cover completely. Mix the glacé cherry pieces and the angelica, and use to decorate across the centre of the cake.

To freeze Either undecorated or finished, this cake freezes beautifully; thaw it for about 2 hours at room temperature.

Note: A deep cake tin 8 inches/ 20 cm in diameter can be used instead of a spring-clip tin; brush the tin with melted fat and line the base with a double layer of kitchen foil. Leave the cake in the tin until it is almost cold, then loosen round the edges and turn it out, but leave the foil under the cake.

The mixture can also be baked in 2, 7-inch/19-cm sandwich tins at *Gas Mark 5 or 375 degrees F or 190 degrees C*, for about 30 minutes.

Apricot and Walnut Loaf

8 oz/250 g dried apricots
2 oz/50 g walnuts
8 oz/250 g plain flour
4 level teaspoons baking powder
8 oz/250 g wholewheat flour
6 oz/175 g butter
8 oz/250 g soft brown sugar
2 eggs, size 2
¼ pint/150 ml milk plus 2 tablespoons
Greaseproof paper
A 2-lb/1-kg loaf tin
FOR THE TOPPING
1 tablespoon clear honey
1 oz/25 g caster sugar
1 oz/25 g butter
1 oz/25 g walnuts, chopped

Brush the tin with melted fat and line the base with a piece of greaseproof paper cut to fit. Brush the lining with melted fat as well.

Chop the apricots and walnuts. Sift the flour into a mixing bowl with the baking powder, then mix in the whole-wheat flour. Rub in the butter and mix in the soft brown sugar, chopped apricots and walnuts. Beat the eggs with the milk and stir them into the dry ingredients.

Turn the mixture into the tin and smooth over the surface. Bake the loaf in a moderate oven, *Gas Mark 4 or 350 degrees F or 180 degrees C*, for 1 hour, then reduce the heat to *Gas Mark 3 or 325 degrees F or 160 degrees C*, for a further hour, if necessary covering the top of the loaf with brown paper. Fifteen minutes before the loaf is ready, melt together the ingredients for the topping and coat the top of the loaf.

Leave the loaf to cool slightly before turning it on to a wire tray to cool completely. Serve cut in thick slices spread with butter.

To freeze Freeze whole or sliced.

Sultana Slices

Makes 16

FOR THE FILLING
3 oz / 100 g butter
2 oz / 50 g soft brown sugar
1 level tablespoon golden syrup
10 oz / 300 g sultanas
1 level tablespoon plain flour
¼ level teaspoon ground cinnamon

FOR THE PASTRY
12 oz / 375 g plain flour
A pinch of salt
3 oz / 100 g lard
3 oz / 100 g margarine

FOR THE GLAZE
1 egg white
A sprinkling of caster sugar
A Swiss roll tin 11¾ inches / 29 cm
   long by 7¾ inches / 19 cm wide

Melt the butter, sugar and syrup in a pan, then stir in the sultanas, flour and cinnamon and bring to the boil, stirring all the time. Simmer for a few seconds then take it off the heat to cool.

To make the pastry Sift together the flour and salt. Add the margarine and lard, cut into small pieces, and rub them into the flour until the mixture resembles fine breadcrumbs. Add just enough cold water to bind the mixture together.

Cut the pastry in half and roll one half into a rectangle to fit the base and sides of the tin. Cover the pastry, lining it with the cold filling. Roll the rest of the pastry to fit the top. Moisten the edges of the pastry in the tin with a little water, lay the top over and press the edges of the pastry together; trim neatly with a knife. Score a trellis pattern over the top of the pastry with the back of a knife.

Beat the egg white for the glaze until it is just frothy and brush it over the surface, then sprinkle the caster sugar lightly over the top.

Bake just above the centre of a hot oven at *Gas Mark 7 or 425 degrees F or 220 degrees C*, for 20 minutes, then lower it to *Gas Mark 6 or 400 degrees F or 200 degrees C*, for a further 15 to 20 minutes.

Cut into triangles while still warm but allow the slices to cool before lifting them out of the tin.

To freeze Freeze in the tin, uncut. It slices best when just thawed.

Triple Decker Squares

Makes 32

FOR THE SHORTBREAD BASE
9 oz / 300 g flour
A pinch of salt
1½ oz / 50 g caster sugar
6 oz / 200 g butter

FOR THE FILLING
8 oz / 250 g butter
8 oz / 250 g soft brown sugar
2 level tablespoons golden syrup
1 (14-oz / 397-g) can full cream
   condensed milk
1 teaspoon vanilla essence

FOR THE TOP
3 oz / 100 g plain chocolate
A deep cake tin, 7 inches / 18 cm
   by 11 inches / 28 cm by 1½ inches /
   3 cm, brushed with melted fat.

Sift the flour and salt into a bowl, add the sugar and rub in the butter. When the mixture resembles fine breadcrumbs, knead it into a ball. Press it well into the base of the tin. Bake it in a moderate oven at *Gas Mark 4 or*

350 degrees F or 180 degrees C, for about 25 minutes. Leave to cool in the tin.

To make the filling Put the butter, sugar, syrup and condensed milk into a pan and stir over a gentle heat until the sugar has dissolved. Bring to the boil and, stirring continuously, boil gently for 7 minutes. Add the vanilla essence, beat well and pour over the shortbread base. Allow to cool before adding the topping.

Break the chocolate into pieces and put them on a plate. Stand the plate over a pan of hot, but not boiling water until the chocolate just begins to melt. Be very careful not to get it too hot or it will streak with white when set. Beat the chocolate with a palette knife to make it smooth, then spread it evenly over the filling.

When the chocolate is quite cold, cut the mixture into approximately 32 squares.

To freeze Freeze in the tray or in neatly cut squares.

Streusel Slices

Makes 16 slices

FOR THE STREUSEL TOPPING
2 oz/50 g plain flour
A pinch of salt
1 level teaspoon cinnamon
2 oz/50 g light brown soft sugar
2 oz/50 g butter or margarine
FOR THE CAKE
4 oz/100 g margarine, softened
4 oz/100 g caster sugar
2 eggs, size 3 or 4
4 oz/100 g self-raising flour
A pinch of salt
2 oz/50 g cut mixed peel
The grated rind of $\frac{1}{2}$ a lemon
An 11 inch/28 cm by 7 inch/18 cm Swiss roll tin, well brushed with melted fat

To make the topping Sift the flour, salt and cinnamon into a bowl, stir in the sugar, then rub in the butter or margarine.

To make the cake Put all the ingredients into a bowl and beat well for 1 minute until the mixture is smooth. Spread the cake mixture in the prepared Swiss roll tin, and sprinkle with topping.

Bake at *Gas Mark 5 or 375 degrees F or 190 degrees C,* for 25 to 30 minutes, and cut into 16 pieces while still warm. Remove from the tin when slightly cooled. The slices keep well in an airtight tin.
Note: This is also delicious eaten warm as a pudding with custard or cream.

To freeze Freeze in the tray or in pieces.

Crusty Lemon Butter Bake

Makes 16 pieces
6 oz/175 g butter, softened
6 oz/175 g caster sugar
2 eggs, size 2
The grated rind of 1 small lemon
6 oz/175 g self-raising flour
A pinch of salt
FOR THE CRUSTY TOP
4 oz/125 g caster sugar
The juice of 1 small lemon
A straight-sided tin 11 inches/
*   28 cm by 7 inches/18 cm by*
*   1¼ inches/3 cm deep, brushed*
*   with melted fat*

Put the butter, sugar, eggs and lemon rind into a bowl and sift in the flour and salt. Beat the ingredients together for 1 minute, or with an electric mixer for just under 1 minute. Turn the mixture into the prepared tin, and smooth over the surface.

Bake in a moderate oven, *Gas Mark 4 or 350 degrees F or 180 degrees C*, for about 40 minutes, when the surface should be soft, though set, and lightly golden. Remove from the oven and, while it is still hot, mix enough caster sugar with the lemon juice to make a thin paste. Spread this over the surface: the lemon juice sinks into the surface leaving the top crispy when it is cold.

Note: The same mixture can be baked in a Swiss roll tin measuring 9 inches/23 cm by 14 inches/35 cm. As the tin is shallower the cake will only take about 30 minutes to bake. Cuts into about 24 squares.

To freeze Freeze in the tray or cut into pieces.

Chocolate Crispies

(Illustrated on page 112)

Cuts into 20 bars
4 oz/125 g golden syrup
4 oz/125 g margarine
4 oz/125 g rice krispies
8 oz/250 g dates, chopped
The grated rind of 1 lemon
A little melted fat
A shallow baking tray measuring
*   11½ inches/28 cm by 7½ inches/*
*   19 cm*
FOR THE TOPPING
6 oz/175 g plain dessert chocolate,
*   in pieces*
1 teaspoon cooking oil

Weigh a small pan on the scales, then pour in the syrup and weigh it, deducting the pan weight. In this way it is easier to be accurate. Add the margarine to the syrup and melt them together over a low heat then stir in the krispies, dates and lemon rind. Mix carefully together. Brush the baking tin with a little melted fat. Press the mixture into the tin as evenly as possible without crushing, then place in the refrigerator for about 2 hours to set.

To make the topping Place the chocolate pieces on a plate over a pan of hot, but not boiling, water and allow to melt. Mix lightly with a palette knife until all the chocolate is smooth; mix in the oil to keep it shiny. Pour the melted chocolate over the mixture in the tin and spread smoothly with a palette knife. Leave in a cool place to harden the chocolate before cutting into 20 bars for serving.

Honey Flapjacks

(Illustrated on page 112)

Cuts into 15 squares

4 oz / 125 g margarine
1 tablespoon honey
4 oz / 125 g light soft brown sugar
8 oz / 250 g rolled oats
A little melted fat
A shallow baking tray measuring
11½ inches / 29 cm by 7½ inches /
19 cm, brushed with melted fat

Put the margarine and the honey into a pan and melt together over a gentle heat. Stir in the sugar and the rolled oats and mix well. Turn the mixture into the prepared tin and spread it evenly with a palette knife or press with the back of a metal spoon. Bake the flapjacks in a moderately hot oven, *Gas Mark 4 or 350 degrees F or 180 degrees C*, for about 20 minutes, until golden brown. Allow to cool slightly and cut into 15 squares while still warm.

Cool completely in the tin, Store in an airtight tin.
Note: For a special occasion icing to pour over the flapjacks, melt together 4 oz / 125 g icing sugar, 4 oz / 125 g butter and 1 tablespoon honey. Pour this icing over the top of the flapjacks and leave to set.

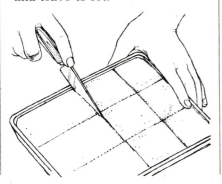

Cinnamon and Almond Biscuits

Makes 24 square biscuits

4 oz / 125 g butter
2 oz / 50 g caster sugar
6 oz / 175 g plain flour
¼ teaspoon ground cinnamon
A pinch of salt
A little milk to glaze
1 oz / 25 g chopped or flaked
almonds
1 oz / 25 g granulated sugar
A Swiss roll tin, 7¾ inches / 19 cm
by 11¾ inches / 29 cm lightly
brushed with melted fat

Beat the butter until soft and creamy. Add the sugar and continue beating until the mixture is light in colour and texture. Sift the flour, cinnamon and salt together then stir them into the mixture. Press the mixture into the prepared tin and flatten with a knife. Brush with milk to glaze and then prick with a fork. Mix the almonds and the granulated sugar together and sprinkle them over the surface.

Bake the biscuits just above the centre of a moderately hot oven, *Gas Mark 4 or 350 degrees F or 180 degrees C*, for about 20 minutes or until it is golden brown. Cut the mixture into 2-inch / 5-cm squares whilst it is still warm and cool in the tin. Store in an airtight tin.

Cut-and-Bake Biscuits

A roll of this biscuit mixture can be kept in the freezer or in the refrigerator ready to slice off and bake.

Makes about 30 biscuits

7 oz/200 g caster sugar
1 egg, size 3
7 oz/200 g plain flour
1 level teaspoon baking powder
½ level teaspoon salt
1 teaspoon vanilla essence
2 oz/50 g chopped nuts
4 oz/125 g butter

Put the sugar into a mixing bowl then stir in the egg with a fork and mix well. Sift the flour into the bowl with the baking powder and salt and stir in the vanilla essence and the chopped nuts. Melt the butter and add it to the mixture to make a soft dough. Knead the dough lightly into a sausage shape, using a little flour to prevent it from sticking; the roll should be about 1 inch/2.5 cm in diameter.

Wrap the dough carefully in greaseproof paper, foil or plastic film and store it in the refrigerator or freezer until a batch is needed. Wrap it in foil as well if you are going to freeze it.

To make biscuits Cut off slices of dough (it will cut straight from the freezer) about ¼ inch/½ cm thick and lay them on a greased baking tray with a little space between each to allow them to spread. Bake the biscuits in a moderate oven, *Gas Mark 4 or 350 degrees F or 180 degrees C*, for about 10 minutes. Cool them on a wire tray.

Note: An easy way to vary this recipe is to use dark, soft brown sugar instead of caster sugar, and chopped raisins instead of nuts.

From a roll of each of these kept in the freezer you can bake a trayful of mixed biscuits whenever you have the oven at the right temperature.

Traditional Shortbread

This quantity will make 3 whole shortbreads.

12 oz/375 g plain flour
A good pinch of salt
8 oz/250 g butter
2 oz/50 g caster sugar
A little extra flour for dusting the mould
A shortbread mould 7 inches/18 cm in diameter

Make sure the mould is clean and dry, then dust with a little flour to coat and tip out the excess flour.

Sift the flour with a good pinch of salt into a large bowl. Cut the butter into small pieces and rub it into the flour with the tips of your fingers. Add the sugar and knead the mixture to a pliable dough just a little softer than that required for a shortcrust pastry. Cut the shortbread dough into 3 even-sized pieces, then use the mould to shape each one in turn. Press the dough into the mould to fill out the pattern then pat with the knuckles to flatten the surface. To loosen it slightly, ease the shortbread dough away from the sides of the mould with a small round-bladed palette knife, then upturn the mould on to an ungreased baking tray, giving it a sharp knock to make the shortbread drop out. Dust the mould again with flour before shaping the other 2 pieces of dough in the same way.

There is no need to brush the baking tray with fat as the shortbread slips off the tray quite easily after baking; the addition of fat might encourage the dough to spread.

Bake the shortbread at *Gas Mark 3 or 325 degrees F or 160 degrees C,* for about 30 minutes, until it is golden brown; allow it to cool and harden slightly before slipping it on to a wire rack to finish cooling. Store in an airtight tin.

Shortbread Biscuits

Makes 36 biscuits
Roll half the Traditional Shortbread mixture to a $\frac{1}{4}$ inch/$\frac{1}{2}$ cm in thickness and cut it into rounds with a 2-inch/5-cm fluted cutter. Make more biscuits, using the rest of the mixture and the scraps. Place the rounds on a baking tray, sprinkle them with caster sugar and bake for about 25 minutes at *Gas Mark 3 or 325 degrees F or 160 degrees C.* Leave on a wire tray to cool. Store in an airtight tin.

Strawberry Cinnamon Shortcakes

(Illustrated on page 111)

Make as for shortbread, sifting 1 level teaspoon of ground cinnamon with the flour. Make and roll the dough, then using a $3\frac{1}{2}$-inch/9-cm round fluted cutter, cut out 6 circles. Then, with a 2-inch/5-cm round fluted cutter, cut out 6 circles. Place circles on a baking sheet and liberally sprinkle with caster sugar. Bake at *Gas Mark 3 or 325 degrees F or 160 degrees C,* for about 25 minutes. Cool on a wire rack.

Arrange halved strawberries over the bases of the larger circles. Top with a little whipped cream and place a smaller shortcake circle on top, dust with icing sugar and decorate with a whole strawberry.

Index

Page numbers in italics indicate illustrations

Almonds:
blanching 11
browning 11
Cinnamon and almond biscuits 123
Anchovy butter 64
Apples:
Apple and blackberry roll 34–5
Apple maraschino 76, 91
Apple sausage rolls 106
Crispy baked pork slices with apples 47
Special baked apples 85
Apricots:
Apricot mayonnaise 67
Apricot and walnut loaf 119
Fresh apricot soufflé 93, 96
Hot apricot soufflé 87
Ratafia apricots 88
Artichokes, globe 21
Artichoke soup, Jerusalem 16
Asparagus:
Asparagus mousse 25
Asparagus soufflé flan 73
Quick asparagus soup 16
Aubergine cheese custard 78
Avocado:
Avocado vinaigrette 22
Creamy avocado starter 22

Bacon:
Carbonara 62
Crispy bacon and herring roes 33
Drunken bacon 48
Quiche lorraine 62, 75
Stuffed marrow rings 77
Bananas:
Banana cream jelly 99
Party bananas 95
Baste, sweet and sour 45
Batter:
Yorkshire pudding 41
Beans:
Bean hot pot 74
Brown bean soup 17
Four-bean salad 81
Béchamel sauce 65
Beef:
Bean hot pot 74
Family meat loaf 44
Hungarian goulash 43
Mince and onions 41
Roast fore rib of beef 40
Salt beef and vegetable soup 43
Salt silverside of beef 43
Steak and kidney stew 42
Steak and mushroom pie 42, 57
Beetroot:
Beetroot and orange salad 80
Buttered beetroot 72
Beurre manié 71
Biscuits:
Cinnamon and almond 123
Cut-and-bake 124
Shortbread 120, 124, 125
Strawberry cinnamon short-cakes 111, 125

Blackberries:
Apple and blackberry roll 84
Blackberry soufflé 97
Blackcurrants:
Blackcurrant mousse 98
Blackcurrant soufflé 97
Kissel 90
blending 9
bouquet garni 9
Brussels sprouts soup 13
Butters:
Anchovy 64
Beurre manié 71
Garlic 65
Herb 65
Hungarian 64
Maître d'hôtel 64
Mustard 65

Cabbage, crispy 71
Cakes:
Chilled rhubarb cheesecake 97
Crusty lemon butter bake 122
Lime and lemon cheesecake 113
Quick chocolate sandwich cake 116
Streusel slices 121
Triple decker squares 120
Cannelloni, stuffed 108
Carbonara 62
Carrots:
Country carrot soup 13
Glazed carrots 72
Cauliflower with cream and herb sauce 74
Celery soup 15
Cheese:
Aubergine cheese custard 78
Baked potato and Parmesan pie 78
Blue cheese dressing 69
Cheese pasta salad 81
Cheese pizza 105
Cheese sauce 108
Cheese scones 115
Ham and cheese fingers 106
Cheese soufflé 59
Cheese, cottage:
Chilled rhubarb cheesecake 97
Crab and cottage cheese flan 39
Cheese, cream:
Lime and lemon cheesecake 113
Liver sausage and cream cheese pâté 18
Cherries:
Cherry Napoleon 101
Cherry sauce topping 98
Coconut and cherry loaf 117
Kissel 90
Chestnuts:
peeling 11
Chicken:
Chicken joints in creamed horseradish sauce 52
Chicken pot-au-feu 53
Crispy oven-baked chicken 51

Lemon-thyme chicken 52
Chiffonade dressing 69
Chocolate:
Chocolate butter icing 116
Chocolate crispies 112, 122
Chocolate strawberry cups 95, 111
Quick chocolate sandwich cake 116
Walnut and chocolate gâteau 1, 118
Chowder, fish 36
Cinnamon:
Cinnamon and almond biscuits 123
Strawberry cinnamon short-cakes 111, 125
Cockle pizza 106
Coconut and cherry loaf 117
Cod:
Cod au gratin 26
Fish chowder 36
Quick kedgeree 34
Coffee 104
Coffee butter icing 116
Coleslaw dressing 68
Coley:
Fish chowder 36
Coquilles St Jacques 38
Crab and cottage cheese flan 39
Cranberry soufflé 97
Cream:
Cream and herb sauce 74
Cream meringue 100
Rum cream with cherry sauce topping 98
Syllabub 99
Cream teas 115
Crispies, chocolate 112, 122
Cucumber and mint salad 81
Custard:
Aubergine cheese custard 78
Norwegian cream 90

Damson soufflé 97
Dill dressing 80
Dressings:
Blue cheese 69
Chiffonade 69
Coleslaw 68
Dill 80
French 67
Green goddess 68
Quick yogurt 68
Tomato 69
Yoghurt 69
Drop scones 114

Eggs:
for baking 114
Buttered egg sauce 66
Curried egg mousse 59
Curry baked eggs 23
keeping 54
Norwegian cream 90
Oeufs sur le plat 56
Onion and egg gougère 61
Pickled eggs 56
Piperade 60
Shirred eggs 56

Fairlop tart 87
Fennel and tomato salad 23, 29

Flans:
Asparagus soufflé 73
Crab and cottage cheese 39
Quiche Lorraine 62, *75*
flan tin, lining 62
Flapjacks, honey *112*, 123
freezing 8
French dressing 67
Fruit:
Kissel 90
Melon fruit salad 109
Fudge icing 116

Garlic 9
Garlic butter 65
Gâteau, walnut and chocolate *1*, 118
Ginger sponge 84
Glacé icing 116
Gooseberry:
Gooseberries and junket 92
Gooseberry soufflé 97
Goulash:
Hungarian 43
Lentil and sausage 49
Grapefruit:
Grilled grapefruit 23
Peppermint grapefruit 22
Gravy 40
Green goddess dressing 68
Greens, brightening colour 70

Haddock:
Fish chowder 36
Quick kedgeree 34
Haddock, smoked:
Lasagne 35
Pancakes 34
Quick kedgeree 34
Ham and cheese fingers 106
Hazelnuts, skinning 11
Herbs:
Cream and herb sauce 74
Herb butter 65
Herrings:
Crispy bacon and herring roes 33
Hollandaise sauce 66
Honey:
Honey flapjacks *112*, 123
Honey icing 123
Hungarian butter 64
Hungarian goulash 43
Huss:
Poisson julienne *2*, 27

Icing:
Butter 116
Chocolate butter 116
Coffee butter 116
Fudge 116
Glacé 116
Honey 123
Lemon butter 116
Orange butter 116

Jelly, banana cream 99
Junket 92

Kedgeree, quick 34
Kidneys:
Devilled kidneys on toast 50
Kidney and sausage turbigo 50
Steak and kidney stew 42
Kissel 90

Lamb:
Bean hot pot 74

Breast of lamb, sweet and sour 45
Devilled kidneys on toast 50
Devon lamb with carrots and cucumber 44
Lamb chop medley 45
Lasagne, smoked haddock 35
Leeks, long *19*, 24
Le Far Breton 83
Lemon:
Crusty lemon butter bake 122
Lemon butter icing 116
Lemon haze 89
Lime and lemon cheesecake 113
Lentils:
Lentil and sausage goulash 49
Red lentils with salt pork 48
Tuna and lentil salad *30*, 37
Lettuce:
Lettuce soup 14
Omelet with lettuce filling 55
Lime and lemon cheesecake 113
Liver:
Liver sausage and cream cheese pâté 18
Stuffed liver 49

Mâitre d'hôtel butter 64
Marrows, stuffed rings 77
Mayonnaise: 67
Apricot 67
Curry 67
Prawn cocktail 68
Melba toast 22
Melon fruit salad 109
Meringue, cream 100
Mincemeat:
Mincemeat jalousie 89
Mince pies 113
Mint and cucumber salad 81
Moules marinières *32*, 38
Mousses:
Asparagus 25
Blackcurrant 98
Curried egg 59
Mushrooms: 10
Devilled mushrooms en cocotte 24
Marinated mushrooms *20*, 25
Mushroom pizza 105
Steak and mushroom pie *42*, *57*
Mussels:
Moules marinières *32*, 38
Mustard:
Home-made mustard 104
Mustard butter 65

Noma Roma 78
Noodles, cooking 50
Norwegian cream 90
Nuts, preparing 11

Oeufs sur le plat 56
Qmelets:
fillings for 55
grilled 54
with lettuce filling 55
Spanish 55
Onions:
chopping 10
dicing 10, *10*
freezing 10
Onion and egg gougère 61
peeling 10
slicing 10
Onions, spring:
Spring onions with peas 71

Spring onion soup 14
Oranges:
Beetroot and orange salad 80
Orange butter icing 116
Orange soufflé 102
peeling 10, *11*
Ox tongue, pressed 51

Pancakes:
Cognac pancakes flambés 88
Smoked haddock 34
with lemon 86
Parsnips:
Curried parsnip soup 15
Glazed parsnips 72
Parties, food for 103–13
Pasta:
Cheese pasta salad 81
Pastry:
Choux 61
Flaky, quick 106
Shortcrust 39, 62, 73, 87, 120
Pâté:
Liver sausage and cream cheese 18
Peaches, skinning 11
Pears:
Fresh pear delight 91
Ratafia pears 88
Upside-down ginger pears 84
Peas:
Spring onions with peas 71
Peppers:
Piperade 60
Pies, pastries and tarts:
Baked potato and Parmesan 78
Fairlop tart 87
Mince pies 113
Steak and mushroom pie 42, *57*
Sultana slices 120
Tuna fish pie 37
Turkey turnover 53
Pig's liver, stuffed 49
Pineapple pudding 82
Piperade 60
Piping 9, *9*
Pizzas:
base, quick recipe 104
basic tomato mixture 104
Cheese 105
Cockle 106
Mushroom 105
Party pizzas 104–6
Tuna 105
Plaice:
Hasty plaice 28
Piquant grilled plaice 28
Ploughman's party 103
Plums:
Fresh plum soufflé 97
Poisson julienne *2*, 27
Pommes boulangères *79*
Pork:
Crispy baked pork slices with apples 47
Glazed pork chops 46
Marinated pork chops 46
Pork and prune casserole 46, *58*
Red lentils with salt pork 48
Rillette of pork 18
Potatoes:
Baked potato and Parmesan pie 78
Creamed potatoes 70

Lemon potato salad 80
Pommes boulangères 79
Potato soup 12
Roast potatoes 40
Pot-au-feu, chicken 53
Pressed ox tongue 51
Prunes:
Pork and prune casserole 46, *58*
Puddings:
Le Far Breton 83
Lemon haze 89
Pineapple pudding 82
Rhubarb and raisin roll 84
Upside-down ginger pears 84
Yoghurt pudding 100
Pumpkin and Tomato Soup 15

Quiche Lorraine 62, *75*

Raisins:
Rhubarb and raisin roll 84
Raspberries:
Brandied raspberries 101
Fresh raspberry soufflé 97
Kissel 90
Ratafia pears 88
Redcurrants:
Kissel 90
Redcurrant soufflé 97
Rhubarb:
Chilled rhubarb cheesecake 97
Rhubarb and raisin roll 84
Rice:
Baked savoury rice 79
Boiled rice 71
Rock salmon:
Poisson julienne *2*, 27
Rum cream with cherry sauce topping 98

Salads:
Beetroot and orange 80
Cheese pasta 81
Cucumber and mint 81
Fennel 29
Four-bean 81
Lemon potato 80
Tomato and fennel 23, *29*
Tomato, with dill dressing 80
Tuna and lentil *30*, 37
Sauces:
Apricot mayonnaise 67
Bacon, onion and mushroom 107
Béchamel 65
Buttered egg 66
Cheese 108
Cherry sauce topping 98
Cream and herb 74
Curry mayonnaise 67
Hollandaise 66
Mayonnaise 67
Prawn cocktail mayonnaise 68
Spaghetti 108

Whipped butter 66
White 66
Sausages:
Apple sausage rolls 106
Kidney and sausage turbigo 50
Lentil and sausage goulash 49
Liver sausage and cream cheese pâté 18
Scallops:
Coquilles St Jacques 38
Scones:
Cheese 115
Drop 114
Sultana 115
Teatime *112*, 115
Treacle 115
Wholewheat 115
Scotch broth 17
Sherry trifle *94*, 110
Shortbread 120, 124, 125
sieving 9
soufflé dish, preparing 102
Soufflés:
Asparagus soufflé flan 73
Cheese 59
Fresh apricot *93*, 96
Hot apricot 87
Hot strawberry 87
Orange 102
Soups:
Artichoke 16
Asparagus, quick 16
Brown bean 17
Brussels sprouts 13
Celery 15
Country carrot 13
Cream of spinach 14
Curried parsnip 15
Fish chowder 36
Lettuce 14
Potato 12
Salt beef and vegetables 43
Scotch broth 17
Spring onion 14
Sweetcorn 14
Ten-minute 16
Tomato and pumpkin 15
Spaghetti, quantities 108
Spaghetti sauce 108
Spinach:
Cream of spinach soup 14
Spinach loaf 72
Sponge, ginger 84
Sprats, grilled 33
Starters:
Asparagus mousse 25
Avocado vinaigrette 22
Creamy avocado 22
Curry baked eggs 23
Devilled mushrooms en cocotte 24
Globe artichokes 21
Grilled grapefruit 23
Liver sausage and cream cheese pâté 18

Long leeks *19*, 24
Marinated mushrooms *20*, 25
Melba toast 22
Peppermint grapefruit 22
Rillete of pork 18
Sweetcorn 21
Tomato and fennel salad 23, *29*
Tuna and lentil salad *30*, 37
Stew, steak and kidney 42
Strawberries:
Chocolate strawberry cups 95, *111*
Fresh strawberry soufflé 97
Hot strawberry soufflé 87
Strawberry cinnamon short-cakes *111*, 125
Strawberry racer 95, *111*
Streusel slices 120
Sultana slices 120
Sweet and sour baste 45
Sweetcorn: 21
Corn and tuna bake 36
Sweetcorn soup 14
Syllabub 99

Tarts, *see* Pies, pastries and tarts
Tea 103
Tomatoes:
basic pizza mixture 104
skinning 11
Tomato dressing 69
Tomato and fennel salad 23, *29*
Tomato and pumpkin soup 15
Tomato salad with dill dressing 80
Traditional shortbread 124
Trifle, sherry *94*, 110
Triple decker squares 120
Tuna:
Corn and tuna bake 36
Tuna and lentil salad *30*, 37
Tuna fish pie 37
Tuna pizza 105
Turkey:
Jubilee turkey *94*, 107
Turkey turnover 53

Vegetables:
Salt beef and vegetable soup 43
Ten-minute soup 16

Walnuts:
Apricot and walnut loaf 119
Walnut and chocolate gâteau *1*, 118
White sauce 66

Yoghurt:
Quick yoghurt dressing 68
Yoghurt dressing 69
Yoghurt pudding 100
Yorkshire pudding 41